preface

this all began with learning how to strip piece with Nancy Crow in 1982; learning to use fabrics as brush strokes of many colors and many values, rather than chunks of just a few of them. It also began by being thunderstruck with the work of Jan Myers-Newbury in the early 1980s; by the way she would use a simple shape and mix color families and values so dramatically . . . over and over again . . . .

With the inspiration of the work of these two artists early in my development as a quiltmaker, I began a journey in strip piecing that led down numerous color avenues. One of these resulted in my developing and teaching the "Strips that Sizzle" approach to quiltmaking, in which students could be guided to make a very simple rotary cut block without first agonizing over fabric choices.

This simple approach helped many students overcome anxiety over putting many colors and many values into a quilt, even if they had never done so before. And, Strips that Sizzle was so much fun to teach and to explore myself, I wanted to come up with other blocks that would be easy enough for quiltmakers just getting started, yet be food for thought for anyone trying to learn more about color and value in quilt-making.

This experimentation led to the discovery of the two basic blocks featured in this book. These blocks are not made of strips, but rather of easy triangles and wedge-shaped pieces; hence the book's name, *Easy Pieces, Creative Color Play with Two Simple Quilt Blocks.*

This book goes far beyond the possibilities presented in the Strips that Sizzle approach, because there is not one but two basic blocks presented here, Block A and Block B. Both are rotary cut and quickly sewn. The basic set of Easy Pieces blocks you make here will include not only the blocks, but mirror image blocks as well. Blocks A and B may be used alone or in combination; you can include their mirror image blocks or not, as you wish. When you add the element of making asymmetrical Block B in reverse value order (along with its mirror image, of course!), you can imagine how the quilt possibilities multiply. In the twenty years I have been actively making quilts, I have never explored a quilt idea that is as versatile as this one is. Every quilt I have made has spawned the ideas for a few others, but no quilt concept has ever spawned dozens of ideas at a time, as Easy Pieces quilts has! Even as I write the last few sentences in this manuscript, there are so many Easy Pieces quilt ideas whirling around in my head, I can hardly wait to get back into the studio to get a few of them out of my swirling brain, and onto the design wall!

And so, dear reader, let's begin . . .

introduction

If you consider yourself timid about using color or value, or if you wish you could use a greater variety of fabrics in your quilts, or if you wish you could stop agonizing about fabric choices, this is the book for you! In these pages you will learn not how to make a single quilt, but rather how to use a simple block as a springboard for numerous quiltmaking possibilities.

Two different blocks—Block A and Block B—are presented herein; each is made up of triangles and wedges. These blocks can be used alone or in combination, and you will be using their mirror images as well to create hundreds of quilts. My goal is to "drop an idea into the pond" of your quiltmaking mind, and encourage you to run with it! Numerous finished quilts are pictured in this book, but they are meant only to whet your appetite for more possibilities for Easy Pieces blocks!

In playing with the blocks described in these pages, you will gain skill in using a wide range of value (all the way up to the lights, and all the way down to the darks) in your quilts. Each of the blocks requires that you use such a range of value, and you will find that your quilt is more successful if you use more fabrics rather than fewer. In these pages you will find techniques to put you at ease in the middle of the quilt shop on sale day, or in the midst of your fabric collection, no matter how large or how small it is. You will learn a lot about fabric color and value—without agonizing. The quilt emerges as you play with these Easy Pieces quilt blocks on your design wall.

You will find the real challenge is to stop playing with the blocks on your design wall and make a quilt with them!

HOW TO USE THIS BOOK

This book's primary chapters concern the following:

1) choosing fabrics with attention to value and techniques for choosing more fabrics rather than fewer
2) the mechanics of making Easy Pieces Blocks A and B
3) patterns derived from rotations of the blocks, alone or in combination
4) design diversions. Thoughts on border and quilting design are also included, as well as how-to instructions for two projects, for those who want more guidance for their first few Easy Pieces quilts.

First, peruse the entire book to get an idea of how the blocks are made, and how they can be rotated to create various designs on the quilt surface. The individual rotation patterns are presented as a menu of motifs from which you can choose to create your own quilt. Easy Pieces quilts are often more interesting if they begin with one pattern, which transforms into another pattern by the time the viewer scans the entire surface of the quilt! This does not mean you cannot use the patterns singly; in such a case, your manipulation of value or use of numerous fabrics may make that single pattern very exciting.

table of
contents

dedication

in loving memory of three dear quilting friends:

Lyn Boland; Issaquah, WA

Bette Kassuba; Richland, WA

Flora Daniel; Prospect, TN

whose lives were cut short by cancer. Their quilts will always bring joy to those they left behind, and the memories of laughter and creative endeavors with them will never dim in the minds of their quilting friends.

acknowledgments

many thanks to so many who have contributed to this book, all the students who have worked with this method so enthusiastically in workshops, and especially to all who sent me photos of their quilts. Thanks to Barb Engelking of The Fabric Works in Superior, Wisconsin, who not only got her students to send me snapshots of the quilts they made as a result of her Easy Pieces workshops, but also introduced me to computer-generated patterns! Most of all, heartfelt thanks to each of the forty-nine quiltmakers who sent work to be photographed for this book.

Thanks to my guild hostesses this year who believed me when I said, "I don't want to be entertained, I just have to sit and write." Highest on this list are Hartley and Marilyn Badger, who left me with only their cat, Hazel, to talk to for one long productive weekend in their beautiful home on the Oregon coast.

Thanks to Mark Frey, quilt photographer extraordinaire . . .your attention to detail is much appreciated!

The writing and publishing of this particular book was due to additional long-term encouragement of two special people, Tom and Carolie Hensley of The Cotton Patch in Lafayette, California. They have been generously supportive of my teaching, my writing, and my quiltmaking from the beginning of my career, almost twenty years ago. They have treated me royally, to be sure. Thank you to Carolie also for loaning tools for the how-to photos, and for providing an ever-changing and ever-expanding selection of cotton fabrics that has kept me "over the top" on my fabric budget for twenty years.

And to all the professional and caring people at C&T Publishing—what a pleasure it is to be a part of your team.

easy
pieces

Creative Color Play with Two Simple Quilt Blocks

Margaret J. Miller

C&T PUBLISHING

Editor: Liz Aneloski
Technical Editor: Cyndy Lyle Rymer
Copy Editor: Judith Moretz
Design Director: Kathy Lee
Book and Cover Designer: John Cram
Illustrator: Kandy Petersen
Photographer of Quilt Images: Mark Frey
Photographer of Cover Quilt and How-to Images: Sharon Risedorph
Published by C&T Publishing, Inc., P.O. Box 1456, Lafayette, California 94549

Cover quilt: *Rainbow Blues* by Margaret J. Miller

Library of Congress Cataloging-in-Publication Data

Miller, Margaret J.
    Easy Pieces : creative color play with two simple quilt blocks /
Margaret J. Miller.
            p.   cm.
            Includes index.
            ISBN 1-57120-051-7
            1. Patchwork.   2. Quilting.   3. Patchwork quilts.   4. Color in textile crafts.   I. Title
TT835.M522 1998
746.46—dc21   98-6315
                                                                                                      CIP

Printed in Hong Kong

10   9   8   7   6   5   4   3   2   1

Next, choose one of the two blocks presented, and make a basic set of blocks following the instructions at the beginning of Chapter One. This basic set will consist of sixteen blocks and sixteen mirror image blocks.

Follow the pattern guidelines presented in Chapter Two, photographing each block arrangement for future reference. Once you have completed the rotations presented in the book, you will have an idea of a direction you would like to go with these blocks. This new direction will probably necessitate making more blocks, but this is an advantage, allowing you to drop out fabrics that didn't work so well, and more importantly, to add more fabrics and/or more values to the original set of fabrics with which you started.

Before settling on a given arrangement of this first set of blocks, make another set of blocks following the basic guidelines as before. For example, if you started with Block A, make a set of Block B. Add these to your Block A set, and go through rotations as before. An organized presentation of these endless possibilities appears in Chapter Three.

SUPPLIES

Cutting Tools

Scissors. Be sure they are sharp for cutting fabric.

Rotary cutter. I use the medium-size wheel. Be sure to have extra blades.

Rotary cutting mat. It should be large enough to cut across the width of a fabric folded selvage to selvage. Mine is 23" x 35".

Acrylic rulers. You will need a 6" x 24" and a 6" square. For larger blocks, you will need a 12" acrylic square. For making filler edge triangles for quilts made of blocks on point, a 15" acrylic square is useful. Acrylic rulers are preferable to plastic ones, since the rotary cutter blades will cut into the plastic.

Designing Tools

Vertical design wall. It is important to play with these blocks on a vertical, not horizontal, surface. My design wall is two four-by-eight foot soundboard panels that are covered with lengths of flannel fabric. The nap of the flannel holds loose quilt pieces in place so I can stand back and evaluate color and design of the developing quilt top. The soundboard can also be pinned into, and doesn't crumble with age like other bulletin board materials such as cork.

You could also use a length of Pellon® fleece or cotton batting tacked to your wall if you do not have room to actually install soundboard panels. There are a number of "fuzzy" surfaces for design walls available for sale in quilt shops; some have square grids printed on them which can be helpful or distracting, depending on your personal taste.

Good lighting. It is imperative in your studio area, whatever it might be.

Reducing glass. A reducing glass or other distancing device is essential for evaluating the design and color of the piece in progress on your design wall, and will also be useful as you peruse the black and white drawings in this book. Reducing glasses are the opposite of magnifying glasses, and can be purchased at art and office supply stores or quilt shops. An alternative device would be binoculars (look through the "wrong" end!) or your camera. Looking through the viewfinder of your camera not only distances you from the quilt, it can eliminate any distracting visual elements in the room around your quilt.

Color wheel. See page 132.

Camera with flash capability. This is helpful to keep track of design layout possibilities.

Number cards. These are useful for keeping track of the photos you take of various arrangements of the blocks (see page 25).

Idea book. This is a loose-leaf or spiral-bound notebook in which you can jot down design ideas as they occur, and keep photos of the various block arrangements you discover en route to your final quilt.

Time. You need to let the design evolve.

Photocopies of patterns. Make photocopies of the block and pattern pages presented in Appendix B (page 134-141). Some of the block maneuvers presented in Chapter Two are easier to do, and easier to see, if you manipulate paper photocopies rather than real blocks. In the quilting chapter you will be playing with quilting designs on paper first by placing tracing paper over the pieced quilt design.

Sewing Tools

Sewing machine. Be sure it is in good running condition and has been recently cleaned and oiled.

Bobbins. You should have five or six filled with appropriate thread. Since all seams are going to be pressed to one side, thread color doesn't matter. I use neutral thread colors for all my machine piecing.

Good steam iron and pressing surface. Use of steam is optional.

Extra ironing board. This is for laying out triangles and wedges in the order in which they will be sewn. For easy retrieval of appropriate shapes, I set this ironing board up to my left, at the same height as and perpendicular to my sewing machine table.

Fabrics. Use good quality, high thread-count cotton fabrics. Occasionally I will use a few of the polyester/cotton blends that have found their way into my fabric collection, but not often. I find printed fabrics are easier to blend with each other than solid-colored fabrics, though a combination of both is acceptable. Stripes and plaids are particularly effective, and a range of print size is often more effective than many similar-size prints.

To get started, I suggest you have at least ¾ yard of each fabric you plan to use. This is a good starting point for your first set of blocks; to make a whole quilt you will need more fabric.

With these tools at hand, it's time to choose fabrics and start cutting!

CHAPTER ONE *making* the blocks

t he quilts in this book are made from two different blocks; Blocks A and B. Both blocks are created from combinations of triangles and wedges, and each block contains six fabrics that move from light to dark in value. The basic set of blocks (either A or B) consists of sixteen blocks and sixteen mirror image blocks.

Block A

Block A Mirror Image

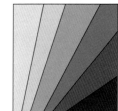

Block B

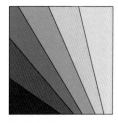

Block B Mirror Image

The directions that follow are for cutting 6" blocks (5½" finished). Cutting directions for blocks of other sizes appear on page 96.

FABRIC SELECTION FOR BLOCKS A and B

Blocks A and B each contain six pieces. As you see in my quilt *Polliwogs* below, it is possible to make Easy Pieces quilts using the same six fabrics in each block. In this quilt, a seventh fabric was used to form the border triangles.

POLLIWOGS
45" X 45"
Margaret J. Miller, 1995
Woodinville, Washington
This quilt has the same six fabrics
in each block, with a seventh fabric
used for the border triangles.

ZIG ZAG
45" X 45"
Martha Houston, 1995
Wichita, Kansas

Using only one color family can be very successful in an Easy Pieces quilt.

Martha Houston also used the same six fabrics in all of the blocks in her quilt *Zig Zag*. The large print used in the corner squares and border was used as a guide for choosing the other fabrics in the quilt.

However, using more than six fabrics enables you to have more variety from block to block, thus more for the viewer to look at in the final quilt. My personal credo is, "Never use two fabrics when you can use twenty," and making quilts from Easy Pieces blocks is a great place to put that into practice!

Therefore, I urge you to choose twelve different fabrics, from each of two color families (e.g., orange/reds and blue/purples). Sort the fabrics by color family into two separate rows, and arrange them from light to dark. To establish a fabric's value location in this row, stagger fabrics so that approximately the same amount of each fabric is visible, and squint your eyes at the grouping so you can focus on the value (lightness or darkness) of the fabric, not its color.

For your first set of blocks you will choose twelve fabrics. Let one color family predominate, but insert three or four fabrics (in their proper value position) from the other color family. Adding these few brings the first color family to life.

Assortment of fabrics laid out by color family.

Fabrics combined into a twelve-fabric grouping.

Twelve fabrics divided into six piles.

Separate these fabrics into six piles of two fabrics each. We will refer to the lightest two fabrics as "Stack 1" and the darkest two fabrics as "Stack 6." Stacks 2, 3, 4, and 5 continue the value gradation; the higher the number, the darker the fabrics.

CUTTING SHAPES FOR BLOCK A

To make Block A, you will cut Stack 1 (the lightest) and Stack 6 (the darkest) into triangles and cut Stacks 2, 3, 4, and 5 into wedge shapes.

To Cut Triangles

Start with Stack 1. Fold each of the two fabrics selvage to selvage. Stack the two fabrics together so the folds and selvages are aligned. Slit the folds up about 6". Align a rotary ruler so you are making a cut perpendicular to the fold (line up one vertical line on the ruler with the folds of the fabric), about 6" from the bottom raw edge. Turn cut strips around, and cut 5½" from newly-cut edge to true it up.

Selvages

Fold

5½"

5½" strip

From this 5½" strip, subcut four 4" segments. The triangles will be cut from these rectangles. Place a straight pin in the leftover fabric, just beyond the last cut. This fabric will then be ready to cut when you need more triangles of these same values.

4"

Leftovers

5½"

Subcut four 4" segments and pin leftovers.

Make a corner-to-corner cut on each of the piles of rectangles. Stack all triangles together (do not separate the individual fabrics).

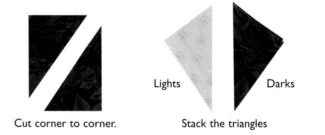

Lights   Darks

Cut corner to corner.   Stack the triangles

Repeat this process with the two darkest fabrics (Stack 6) as shown above. Stack the leftovers together in an area of your work table where they can be easily retrieved when you need more triangles of these fabrics.

After cutting each stack of fabrics, fold the leftover yardages together so you remember which two fabrics were in each of your six stacks. Store these together with the pinned leftovers from your triangles.

To Cut Wedges

Take each of your four remaining piles of fabrics in turn, and cut wedges as follows.

Fold the fabrics selvage to selvage. Stack the fabric pairs on the cutting table with folds and selvages aligned. Slit the folds up a little more than 9". With a vertical line of the ruler aligned with folds, crosscut a little beyond 9" of fabric; turn this strip around and trim to 9". From this 9" strip subcut two 3½" segments and two 3" segments. Place a pin in the leftover fabric.

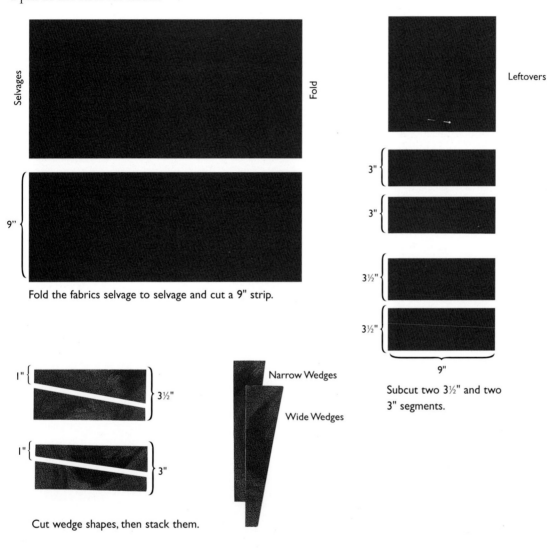

Fold the fabrics selvage to selvage and cut a 9" strip.

Cut wedge shapes, then stack them.

Subcut two 3½" and two 3" segments.

Place the resultant shapes so they are horizontal rectangles in front of you. From each of these four piles of rectangles, cut wedge shapes by placing the ruler about one inch down from the upper left-hand corner of the rectangle, and about one inch up from the lower right-hand corner. Check before you cut—make sure it is a wedge shape you are cutting, not some other geometric form!

Place the wedges cut from the 3½" rectangles in one pile—these we will call the "wide" wedges. Place those cut from the 3" rectangles in another pile—these will be called the "narrow" wedges. Stagger the two piles of wedges, one on top of the other.

Special Cutting Instructions for Striped Fabrics

Striped fabrics are especially effective in Easy Pieces quilts. If you use a stripe, you have a couple of extra decisions to make. Do you want the stripe to go lengthwise (parallel to the straight-grain edge) or crosswise on your wedge shape?

To achieve these effects, you need to use different cutting procedures depending on whether the stripe is printed parallel to the selvages or perpendicular to them.

Stripes Printed Perpendicular to Selvages

If you cut your wedges as explained in the general directions on pages 13, the stripes will end up "crosswise" on your wedge.

Lengthwise or Crosswise?

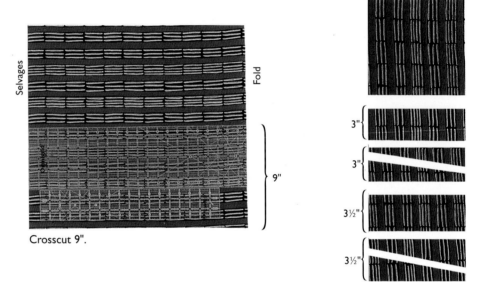

Crosscut 9".

Subcuts made; wedge shapes cut.

If you want your stripes to go lengthwise on the wedge, lay the fabric out folded selvage to selvage, and crosscut 14" of fabric. Next, subcut two 9" sections; stack one of them on top of the other. Then subcut two 3½" x 9" rectangles, and two 3" x 9" ones; from these you will cut your wedge shapes.

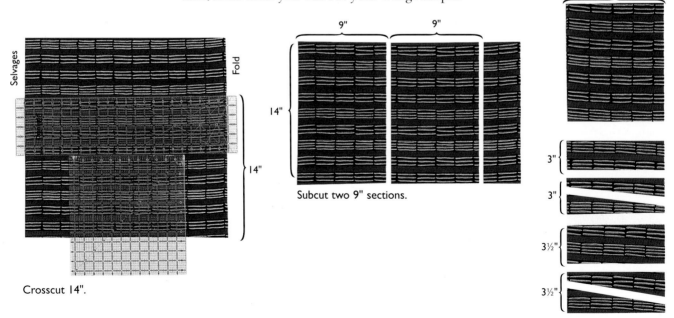

Crosscut 14".

Subcut two 9" sections.

Subcuts made; wedge shapes cut.

Stripes Printed Parallel to Selvages

If you cut your wedges according to the general instructions given on page 13, your stripes will end up lengthwise on your wedge shape.

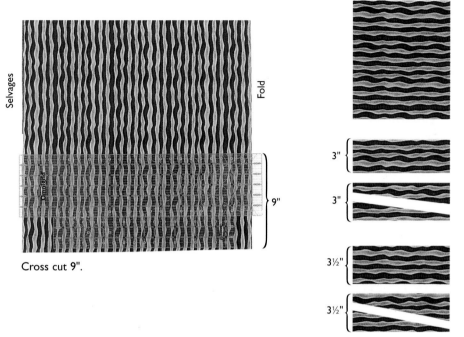

Cross cut 9".

Subcuts made; wedge shapes cut.

If you want your stripes to be crosswise on the wedge, lay out the fabric folded selvage to selvage, and crosscut 14" of fabric. From this, subcut two 9" sections; stack and align them one on top of the other. Subcut two 3" x 9" rectangles and two 3½" x 9" rectangles. Stack respective sizes on top of each other; cut wedge angle.

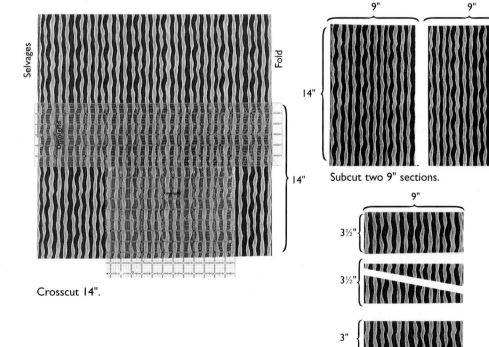

Crosscut 14".

Subcut two 9" sections.

Subcuts made; wedge shapes cut.

Blocks and Their Mirror Images

Remember that these wedges and triangles will be used to create not only blocks, but mirror image blocks as well. To determine which is a block and which is its mirror image (whether you're making Block A or Block B), place your hand on the block (or on stacks of triangles and wedges arranged in the order in which they will be sewn together) so your wrist is in the corner of the block where the narrowest ends of the wedges are, and your thumb falls into the dark triangle. If it is your left thumb that is in the dark triangle, your hand is on a block. If it is your right thumb that is in the dark triangle, your hand is on a mirror image block.

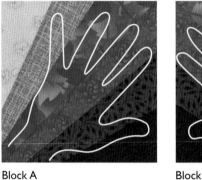

Block A

Block A Mirror Image

Block B

Block B Mirror Image

ARRANGING WEDGES AND TRIANGLES FOR SEWING

Note that the wedges have a straight-grain edge and a bias edge. Whenever you have a bias edge to sew, you will have less problem with that bias edge stretching if you sew it to a straight-grain edge. Also, if you put these two fabrics into the sewing machine in such a way that the bias edge is against the feed dogs, you will have less distortion of your seam. You are going to set up your triangles and wedges so you automatically sew a bias edge to a straight-grain edge, and the bias edge will always be against the bed of the machine and the feed dogs.

Part of the appeal of the Easy Pieces blocks is that there is variety from block to block—they don't look like there was a specific template for every shape. This is why you have cut "wide" wedges and "narrow" ones. You will want to set up the wedges in such a way that you will automatically alternate a wide wedge with a narrow one in each block.

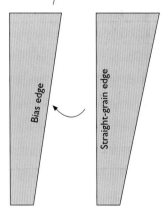

Bias edge

Straight-grain edge

The wedges have a bias edge and straight-grain edge.

Set your wedges and triangles on the table with light triangles on the left, wedges arranged lighter to darker left to right, and darkest triangles on the right. Be sure the straight-grain edge of the wedge is on the left. Stagger your wide wedges and narrow wedges according to the photo below. You will sew your blocks first, then their mirror images.

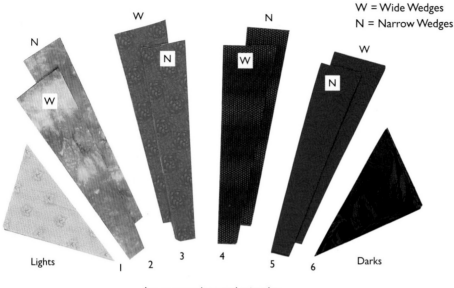

Arrange wedges and triangles.

SEWING BLOCK A

The most efficient and fastest way to sew these shapes together is to "chain piece" them using a scant ¼" seam. This means you will sew the shapes from two consecutive piles one after the other, without breaking your threads in between. You will be sewing all the wedges together first, then adding the triangles.

Beginning with wedge Stacks 2 and 3; bring them within easy reach of your sewing machine. Place a wedge from Stack 3 right sides together with the topmost wedge of Stack 2.

Match the wedges at the narrower end; sew from the wider to the narrower end of the wedge. Do not break the thread.

The wedges may or may not match at the top (wider) ends; it doesn't matter, because the beginnings and endings of all these seams will be trimmed away when the block is squared up.

NOTE: It is very important that you place the wedges right sides together in the same manner as you would turn the pages of a book; the wedge from the right-hand stack (page 2) is always on top (page 1). Make sure the "new page" wedge is on top as you put the wedges through the sewing machine.

Triangles and wedges laid out ready for sewing.

First two piles of wedges, first two wedges in place for sewing.

First wedges under presser foot; two wedges for mirror image block flipped out of the way.

Taking a pair of wedges off top of stack and placing on bottom of same-width stack.

Note that the next two wedges in the stack are wrong side up; these will be sewn together later for the mirror image blocks. Flip them over onto the table (they will now be right side up), placing them directly above the wedge piles from which they came. Now pick up the next pair of wedges; place a wedge from Stack 3 onto a wedge from Stack 2, match at the narrower end, and sew from the wider to narrower ends of wedge shapes.

If you continue in this fashion, sewing one pair of wedges and flipping the next "wrong side up" out of the way, you will end up with two distinct sets of blocks. Six fabrics will always end up together in one set of blocks, and the remaining fabrics will all end up in the second set of blocks.

To build more variety from block to block, every so often take a PAIR of wedges off the right-hand pile and place it on the bottom of its same-width stack. This will give you a new combination of fabrics to sew together. Do this about twice in the process of sewing the narrow wedges and about twice while sewing the wider wedges to their mates in the left-hand pile.

Be sure to take a pair of wedges from the right-hand stack of wedges only, and be sure to place them on the bottom of their same-width stack.

Continue in this manner, sewing a pair of wedges, flipping a pair, and occasionally taking a pair of wedges to put on the bottom of their same-width pile. Keep sewing and flipping until there are no more wedges in Stacks 2 and 3.

Now go back to the beginning of your string of sewn wedges and open the first pair you sewed together. Take the first wedge from Stack 4, sew it right sides together to Wedge 3. Do not break the thread; flip the "wrong side up" wedge out of way, sew the next wedge to the next pair on the string, and so on until Stack 4 is all gone. Don't forget—every so often, take a pair of wedges off the top of Stack 4 and put them on the bottom of their same-width pile.

It is important to keep the wedges in order so you automatically sew alternate wide and narrow wedges in any grouping. If you don't clip threads between groups of wedges at some point, the wedges may become badly tangled and awkward to sew together. As you begin to add a new pile of wedges onto your string of sewn ones, you may clip the threads between the pairs of wedges as you come to them, but clip off only one at a time. The new continuous thread that is sewing Wedge 4 onto Wedges 2 and 3 will keep your string of wedges in order.

Sew wedges from Stack 5 to the groups of three wedges already assembled in the same fashion. Don't forget to go back to the beginning of your string of wedges before beginning to sew a new pile.

After all the wedges are sewn together it is no longer necessary to keep them in order while you add the triangles to the finished wedge groups.

Sew light triangles onto the lightest wedge, dark triangles onto the darkest wedge. For Block A, triangles should be placed about 1" up from the narrowest part of the wedge.

When you sew the dark triangles, you will be sewing bias to bias, but if you sew slowly and with the triangle against the bed of the machine, distortion of the bias edges shouldn't be a problem.

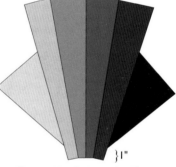

Sew a triangle to each side of the wedge section 1" up from the base.

As with the wedges, one triangle will be "right side up" in the pile, the next will be "wrong side up." Just flip the "wrong side up" triangle out of the way as you did for the wedge shapes. You can pick and choose so you mix up the fabric combinations you sew together (in other words, don't always sew the same fabric triangle to the same wedge fabric).

Sewing the Mirror Image Block A

Bring the mirror image stacks of triangles and wedges toward you. Do not turn anything around, or turn anything over! Take a wedge from Stack 3 (straight grain of the wedge should still be on the left) and sew it to a wedge from Stack 2.

You will now sew from the narrower end to the wider end of the wedge.

Finish sewing wedges from Stacks 2 and 3.

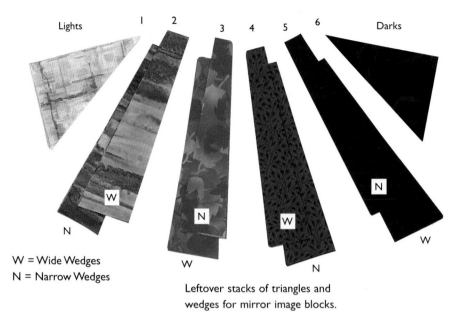

Lights   1   2   3   4   5   6   Darks

W = Wide Wedges
N = Narrow Wedges

Leftover stacks of triangles and
wedges for mirror image blocks.

Sewing mirror image shapes together is a faster process than sewing the block shapes, because it is the narrow end of the wedge you match before you sew, and there is nothing "wrong side up" to flip out of the way anymore. Furthermore, you have already mixed up your fabric combinations, so you don't have to think about that either.

Continue adding wedges from Stack 4, then Stack 5, and finally, add a triangle to each side of the wedge section (light triangle on the light wedge, dark triangle on the dark wedge).

Pressing the Blocks

Press the blocks from the wrong side first, with all the seam allowances pressed in one direction, toward the dark triangle. Then press from the right side as well, so you have a very flat pieced fabric from which to cut your quilt block. Be gentle with the blocks as you press them, and when you play with them on your design wall. Remember, they have all bias edges!

Cutting Out Block A

Place a 6" square acrylic ruler onto the assembled triangles and wedges so two opposite corners are on the middle seam. Place the template as close to the edge of the narrow ends of the wedges as possible; this way you will get the most of your lightest and darkest values into the block. Trim two sides of the square; rotate and cut the other two sides. The rotary mats that are on lazy Susan trays are particularly helpful for cutting these blocks. Or, use a small mat you can rotate rather than disturbing the block to cut the opposite two sides.

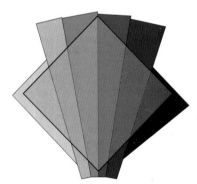

Place 6" square acrylic ruler
onto assembled triangles and
wedges with opposite corners
on middle seam.

CUTTING SHAPES FOR BLOCK B

Block B is an asymmetrical block; it is made of five wedges and one triangle. The triangles are cut in the same fashion as for Block A (pages 11-12). Values 2, 3, 4, and 5 are cut into wedges just as these values were cut for Block A (page 13).

The only shape cut differently is the lightest value; it is a wedge shape and is cut into wider wedges only. (Do not cut narrower wedges of your lightest values.)

In other words, stack your lightest values on the cutting surface with folds and selvages aligned. Slit folds up a little more than 9". Crosscut and true up a 9" strip. Subcut this strip in 3½" segments ONLY: Do not cut any 3" segments of these lightest values for Block B. Cut 3½" rectangles into wedges as described on page 13.

ARRANGING SHAPES AND SEWING BLOCK B

Lay out the wedges and triangles according to the photo below, with the straight grain on the left, alternating stacks of wide and narrow wedges in Stacks 2, 3, 4, and 5. Begin sewing wedges from Stacks 1 and 2, placing a wedge from Stack 2 right side down onto a wedge from Stack 1 (like turning pages of a book). Match the narrow ends of the wedges and sew from the wider end of the wedge to the narrower end. Be sure Wedge 2 is on top as they go through the machine. Do not break the machine threads. Flip the next pair of "wrong side up" wedges from these piles out of the way, and sew the next pair of wedges together.

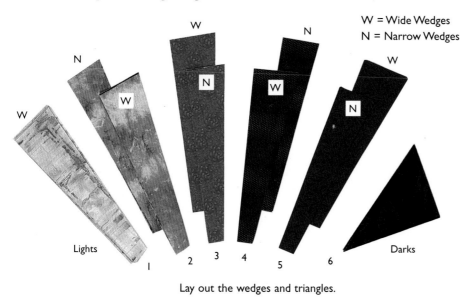

Lay out the wedges and triangles.

As in Block A, every so often take a pair of wedges off the right-hand stack of wedges and put it to the back of its same-width stack. When all wedges of Stacks 1 and 2 have been either sewn or flipped out of the way, go back to the beginning of your string of sewn wedges; sew a wedge from Stack 3 onto the Stack 2 wedge in your first pair of sewn wedges.

Continue in this fashion until all wedges have been sewn together, or flipped out of the way.

Match long point of triangle to narrower end of darkest wedge.

Remember: The new wedge you reach for should be on top as the pair of wedges go through your sewing machine.

Sew the triangles for the B blocks to the darkest wedges by matching the long point of the triangles to the narrower ends of the darkest wedges.

Sewing Mirror Image Block B

Pull the remaining stacks of wedges and triangles toward you without turning anything over or turning anything around! The straight-grain edge of the wedges should still be on the left. Sew the wedges from Stack 2 onto the wedges of Stack 1, sewing from the narrower end of the wedge toward the wider end. Do not cut the machine threads between the pairs of wedges. When all of Stacks 1 and 2 have been sewn, go back to the beginning of the string of sewn wedges and add the wedges of Stack 3, in order, to the wedges already sewn together. Sew the darkest triangles onto the wedges, matching the long point of the triangle to the narrower end of the darkest wedge.

Pressing Block B

Press from the wrong side first with all the seam allowances pressed toward the dark triangle; then press from the right side.

Cutting Out Block B

Block A has a seam going through two of the block's corners, dividing the block in two. In Block B, no seams pierce its corners.

Place 6" square acrylic ruler onto assembled triangles and wedges with template edge parallel to straight-grain edge of lightest wedge. The first fabric should form a wedge, (as shown above)not a stripe (as shown below).

Place a 6" square acrylic ruler onto the assembled triangles and wedges so that its edge is parallel to the straight-grain edge of the lightest wedge. Move the square down to create the the largest dark triangle possible. Double check to see that the upper-right corner of the square has not shifted over too close to a seam. You may need to slide the square up a little, or rotate it slightly, to keep the corner away from the seam.

The important thing is that the first fabric should form a wedge of light in the block, not a stripe of light.

Cut two sides, rotate the entire piece, and cut the other two sides.

If you are making a quilt that will consist of only B blocks (no A blocks), you can cut Block B a little larger than six inches. The wedges and triangles you have cut and sewn together will easily accommodate a 6½" block, sometimes even a 7" block, if you have narrow seam allowances.

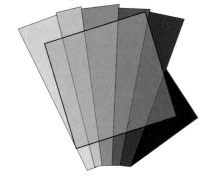

RAINBOW BLUES
54" X 64"
Margaret J. Miller, 1996
Woodinville, Washington

This quilt was begun in an effort to use up the leftovers from *Go for the Green*, pictured on page 103.

In my quilt *Rainbow Blues*, I took advantage of this leeway to make rectangular blocks for the border rows. Instead of cutting a 6" square from the assembled wedges and triangle, I cut a rectangle 6" x 6½". The corner blocks were 6½" square. This procedure seems to give the quilt some breathing room, plus it allows the red color to occasionally "escape" into the border.

BLOCK B: THE REVERSAL BLOCK

Block B is an asymmetrical block. (Block A is symmetrical, since the corner-to-corner seam divides the block into two parts, each with two wedges and one triangle.) Because Block B is asymmetrical, it can be made in a reverse form. In other words, instead of ranging from light to dark from first wedge to triangle, it can be made in the reverse value order. The darkest value would be the first wedge, graduating in value so that the lightest value is in the triangle.

Block B

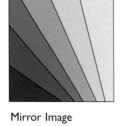
Mirror Image

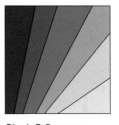
Block B Reverse

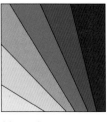
Mirror Image

Wedges 2, 3, 4, and 5 are cut exactly as they were for Block B. For the reversal block, however, the lightest values are cut into triangles, and the darkest values are cut into the wide wedges only. When the wedges and triangles are laid out on the table ready to be sewn, they look like this:

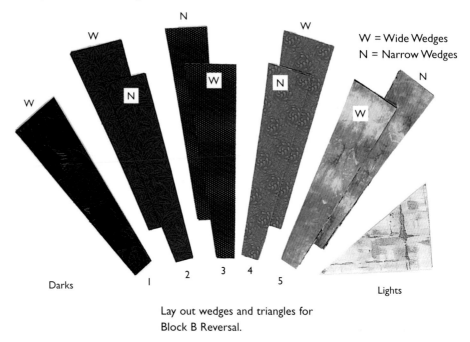

W = Wide Wedges
N = Narrow Wedges

Darks   1   2   3   4   5   Lights

Lay out wedges and triangles for
Block B Reversal.

Follow the same piecing, pressing, and cutting out procedure as described for Block B (pages 21-22).

Once your basic set of blocks has been made, the real fun begins: playing with them on the design wall! Remember that they have all bias edges, so handle them gently!

CHAPTER TWO creating quilts
with easy pieces blocks

So many quilt possibilities exist from arranging and rearranging these blocks that your challenge will be to stop playing with the blocks on the design wall and sew them into a quilt! To get a glimpse of how vast the possibilities are, make a set of blocks and place them in the arrangements that follow. The basic cutting directions given on pages 11-22 will yield sixteen blocks and sixteen mirror image blocks. This is the minimum number you should have to try the block arrangements which follow; however, the more blocks you have, the better idea you have of the potential of each arrangement.

Take a snapshot of each arrangement of blocks on the design wall, and you will have a ready visual reference of the possibilities. Later, you can combine two or more of these arrangements into your quilt design. Fill the camera's viewfinder frame with your block arrangement, and always stand at the same distance from your design wall to take the photograph.

I do not recommend that you use a Polaroid® camera and film. Use your regular camera and print film with a flash. The colors are more true, and most drug stores offer "two for one" developing of the prints and one-hour or overnight service. Multiples of the same photographs are handy quilt design tools.

As you work with the blocks, you will stumble onto wonderful arrangements of them; if you do not take a photograph of such arrangements, you may move two quilt blocks and never be able to get back to the original design again without a photograph to go by!

Photographs are also useful for seeing your block arrangement upside down, sideways, or on point. Never assume that the way you arrange your blocks on the wall is right side up for the final quilt!

Make a set of large numbers to photograph along with each block arrangement. I draw these numbers on 5" x 7" index cards with a thick magic marker; each number fills a single index card. As you take each photo, pin the number card to the upper-left corner of the block arrangement. In a notebook, make notes on the numbered arrangements you photograph. For example, you may sketch in the "shorthand version" of the blocks, or make a note to yourself to try another variation at some future point. You may define the block arrangement in terms of previous arrangements, such as "this is arrangement #7 with every other row turned upside down." As you look back at your photographs, your notes become inspirations for future quilts!

THE PATTERNS

The block arrangements that follow do not represent all of the possible ways Easy Pieces blocks can be combined in a quilt; they are intended only as a menu of motifs from which to choose to create your quilt. Also, they are meant to help you avoid agonizing over how you are going to arrange your blocks on the wall. Using these arrangements, you will get your blocks onto the design wall as quickly as you can. Then you can go back and fine tune your block placement choices.

Many of these arrangements may seem very simple and predictable; however, I have found that when you are trying to explore a design idea, it is important to go back to the simplest form of the design idea you are working on. Moreover, some of the simplest block arrangements can be made dramatic by the movement of value or using a large number of fabrics in a given quilt. (See *Sunrise, Sunset* on page 76, which is Pattern Two viewed sideways!)

The charts that accompany the following quilt illustrations use arrows to indicate the block direction; the arrows point toward the widest part of the wedge. A plain arrow represents a block; an arrow with a black dot at the base represents a mirror image block. The first arrangements are of blocks only, and the same arrangement is shown with both Blocks A and B, so you can see how different these blocks look in the same pattern. There will be more differences in some rotations than in others. Be sure to look at these block arrangements through your reducing glass, as well as with the naked eye.

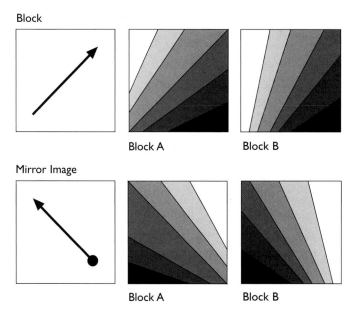

Along with the discussion of individual patterns, maneuvers that can transform these basic patterns will be presented. These include offsetting motifs, using directional patterns in more than one direction, etc., and should be considered in the process of quilt design. For example, if you have a regular repeat pattern, let the pattern be a regular repeat in part of the quilt, offset in other areas.

Throughout the rest of the book, these arrangements will be referred to by the numbers with which they are listed here.

Blocks Positioned as Squares

Pattern One
All Blocks in One Direction

This may seem like too simple a starting place, but it is a good illustration of the difference between Blocks A and B. Note that there is much more light in the B block; this is because the first and second wedges are lights. The A block presents a much more equal distribution of lights and darks.

Pattern One: Block Rotation   Block A   Block B

Pattern Two
Even Horizontal Rows Rotated One-Quarter Turn

Though the A block forms a regular overall pattern, note the horizontal stripe, almost a horizon line, formed by the first (lightest) wedge of the B block. Turn the book 90 degrees clockwise; now notice how the row in which the light wedges line up appears to advance toward the viewer.

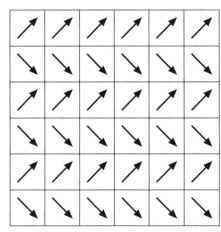
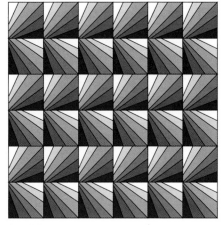
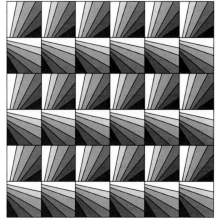

Pattern Two: Block Rotation   Block A   Block B

Pattern Three
Even Horizontal Rows Rotated One-Half Turn

Note that in the A block, a "keg shape," or repeat oval appears; in some blocks, a parallelogram that slants to the right is more obvious. In the B block, on the other hand, the wedges look like strands of ribbons that have been twisted in the middle.

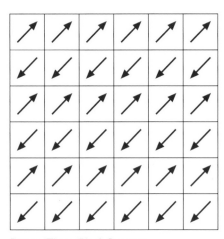

Pattern Three: Block Rotation

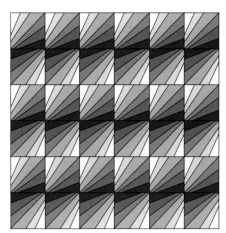

Block A

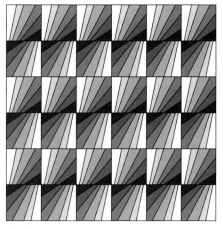

Block B

Pattern Four
Even Horizontal Rows Rotated Three-Quarter Turn

This rotation produces "flying geese heading west." But note that in the A block, the triangles are much more distinct. The change in the angle in the B block makes a much more fluid angle. The triangles seem to be like the fronts of ducks, with ripples in the pond ahead of them as they swim to the left.

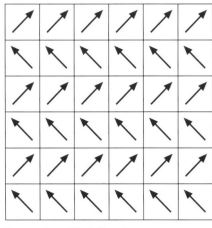

Pattern Four: Block Rotation

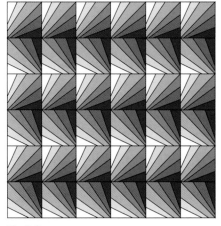

Block A

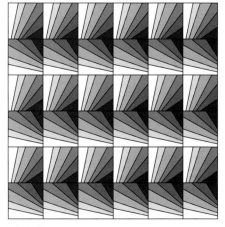

Block B

Pattern Four is the first example of a directional pattern. Whenever you discover a directional pattern, think about using that pattern in more than one direction in the quilt. Below are just two examples of how this pattern could be used in two directions (left) or all four directions (right).

Pattern Four, multiple directions.

Variations on Patterns One through Four
Rotating Vertical Rows of Blocks

Another basic variation on the simplest theme of all (all blocks oriented the same direction) is to rotate every other vertical row by one-quarter turn. In some cases, the pattern is the same as those already described, but the whole grouping has been rotated one-quarter turn.

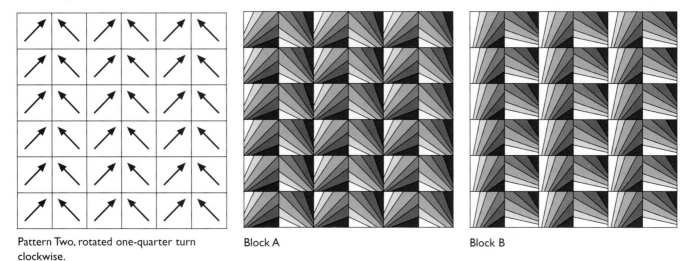

Pattern Two, rotated one-quarter turn clockwise.

Block A

Block B

The Block A arrangement above is the pattern for my quilt *Sunrise, Sunset* pictured on page 76.

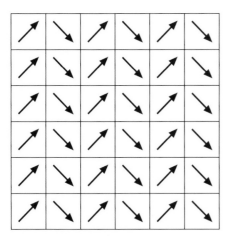

Pattern Four, rotated one-quarter turn clockwise.

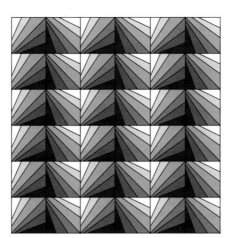

Block A

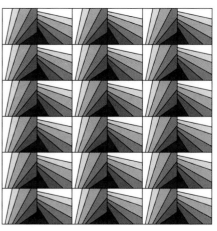

Block B

Pattern Five

Parallelograms and Twisted Ropes

When you turn every other vertical row upside down, a new pattern emerges, which suggests strong parallelograms, especially with the A block. A softer, "twisted rope" image emerges in the Block B grouping.

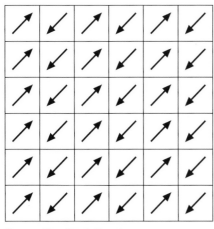

Pattern Five: Block Rotation

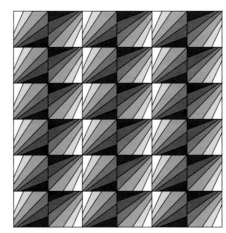

Block A

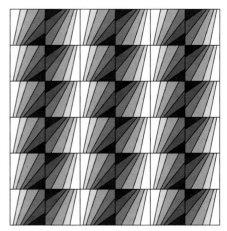

Block B

Pattern Six
Repeat Light Stars or Rounded Diamonds

Note that to achieve this pattern, in each group of four blocks the arrows go counter-clockwise around the center.

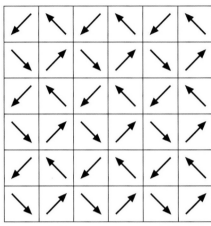

Pattern Six: Block Rotation

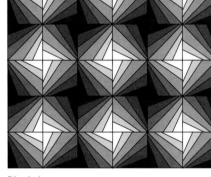

Block A

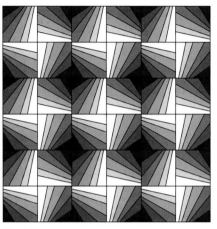

Block B

Pattern Seven
Repeat Dark Stars

This pattern is the reverse of Pattern Six, since the arrows in each group of four blocks go clockwise around the center.

Place two pieces of paper onto Pattern Six so you block out the top horizontal row and the left-hand vertical row; now you have Pattern Seven! You now see that Patterns Six and Seven are the same design; however, note that where you start and stop the pattern determines what motif becomes more obvious (light diamonds vs. dark stars).

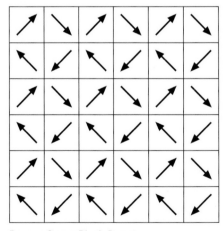

Pattern Seven: Block Rotation

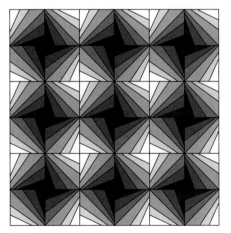

Block A

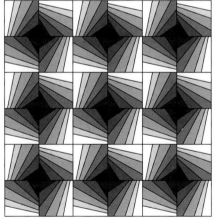

Block B

Another pattern maneuver that would end in the same result with Patterns Six and Seven is to take a row of blocks and put it on the other side of the arrangement on the wall. In other words, take the top row of blocks and put it on the bottom; or, take a side row of blocks and put it on the other side. This maneuver may yield an entirely different pattern.

Patterns Six and Seven are examples of motifs that line up in rows. Whenever you work with patterns like this, try offsetting the motifs from each other in part of the quilt. Note the zigzag that emerges when these are offset from each other.

Pattern Six, offset.

Pattern Seven, offset.

In my quilt *Persimmon*, a regular checkerboarding of red and blue patterns is given a new look when the "checkers" are offset from each other, thus looking more like stacked blocks. When you offset patterns, it is often necessary to fill in the gaps at the ends of the offset rows with partial motifs (note row four from the top of the quilt; two half-motifs flank two whole motifs in this row).

PERSIMMON

63½" X 77½"

Margaret J. Miller, 1997

Woodinville, Washington

Machine quilted by Patsi Hanseth,

Mt. Vernon, Washington

This is the first Easy Pieces quilt I ever made;

its blocks were cut as 7" squares.

Another maneuver you can perform is to combine whole motifs with half motifs for an interesting quilt design. Below are just two of the many examples possible using Patterns Six and Seven.

Pattern Six, combining whole motifs and half motifs.

Pattern Seven, combining whole motifs and half motifs.

If we take this maneuver one step farther and start using quarter motifs, in combination with whole and half motifs, the following quilt plans emerge.

Pattern Six, combining whole motifs, half motifs, and quarter motifs.

Pattern Seven, combining whole motifs and half motifs.

Pattern Eight
Arrows and Zigzags

This pattern is one of several examples in which the same arrangement of Blocks A and B look very unlike each other. Note that there is a strong diamond pattern to the overall field of the A Blocks, while the light wedges in Block B form a diagonal zigzag pattern.

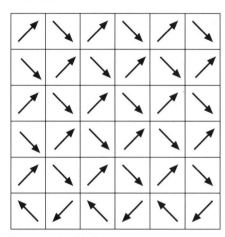

Pattern Eight: Block Rotation

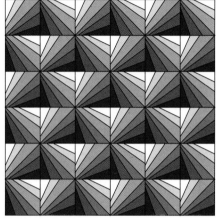

Block A

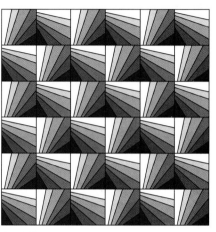

Block B

In the Block B version, the zigzag is a directional pattern; therefore your first option is to use that zigzag in multiple directions in the quilt.

On the left, below, squinting your eyes reveals that the zigzag is used in two directions. On the right, the photocopy from the illustration on the left was cut in four; when two of the resulting four groups of blocks are rotated, a diamond shape is formed with the directional zigzags.

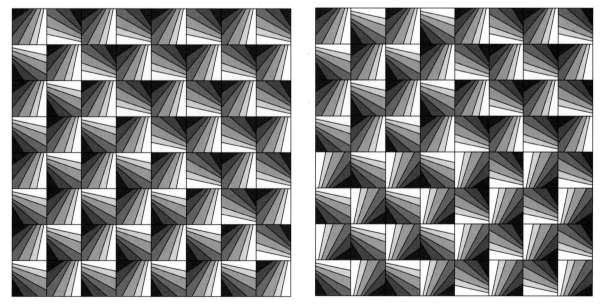

Pattern Eight Block B, zigzag in multiple directions.

With this pattern we introduce another strategy; making a paper "window" in order to select areas of the overall pattern to highlight with value or color. This window is effective only with Block A, because of its symmetry. The edges of the window are the corner-to-corner lines that divide Block A in half.

To make a window, make two photocopies of Pattern Eight from page 35. Glue one photocopy to a piece of file folder cardboard. With a rotary cutter, cut out four "sections" as in the diagram below. Turn the photocopy over, and you now have a "window" that you can move around over the other photocopy, as well as other Block A patterns to isolate different designs.

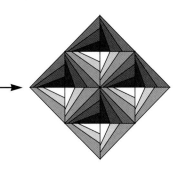

Blocks removed to create window.

Making a paper window.

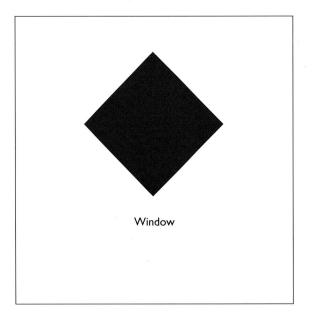

Window

Pattern Eight yields only one design using this method. However, note that it is a directional design. By turning this unit different ways, you can produce multiple quilt designs using Pattern Eight as your jumping-off place.

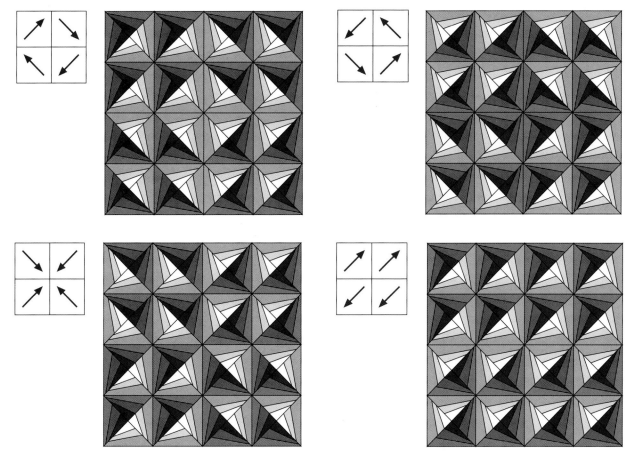

Pattern Eight, four window units rotated.

Pattern Nine
Hourglasses

This pattern was derived by isolating the directional motif in the window unit of Pattern Eight and using it in multiple directions. When you squint at this pattern as Block A, you see light hourglasses, positioned both horizontally and vertically. This is another good pattern to use with the "window" you made for Pattern Eight; in this case, two different motifs can be isolated.

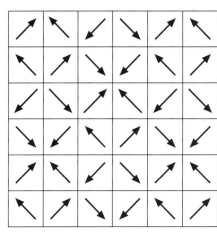

Pattern Nine: Block Rotation

Block A   Block B

Pattern Nine, two motifs isolated.

The hourglasses are not so obvious in Block B, but by isolating parts of the design other patterns emerge. Note that there is a pinwheel motif (at left) which could be highlighted with various colors and/or values, or crossed diagonal swirling ribbons (at right).

Pattern Nine, pinwheel motif.

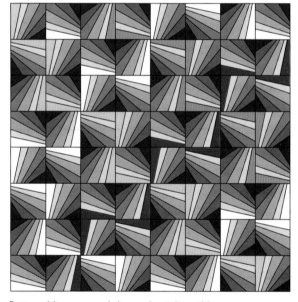

Pattern Nine, crossed diagonal swirling ribbons.

Pattern Ten
Harlequin Diamonds and Dancing Pinwheels

This is another pattern that looks very different depending on whether it is made with Block A or Block B. When you squint your eyes at the illustrations below, Block A yields a crisp harlequin diamond effect, while Block B produces a more fluid design of dancing light pinwheels.

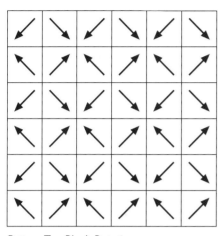

Pattern Ten: Block Rotation

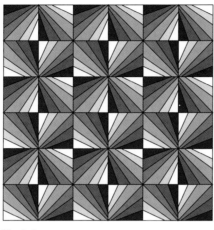

Block A

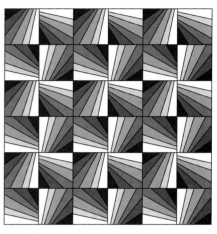

Block B

JAZZ DANCE
67" X 78"
Janet Renfro, 1996
Johnson City, Tennessee

This quilt is based on Pattern Ten, made very effective by keeping red in the body of the quilt only.

This is the pattern Janet Renfro used in the body of her quilt *Jazz Dance* (page 39). The addition of red as an accent brings this crisp pattern to life even more. Janet's choice of border for this quilt is particularly effective. Placement of the lightest triangles at the edge of the quilt makes it look like the colorful middle floats on a light background.

Pattern Ten, Block A yields a couple of "window motifs." One has a star-like quality, while the other has a roundness.

Pattern Ten, two motifs isolated.

Alternating these motifs in a row makes an interesting border of two rows of diamonds that seem to float above a flowing river of light and dark.

Look what happens when we cut this border apart on the lines indicated, and turn every other section upside down! It is obviously more efficient to play with paper photocopies of these blocks for this kind of maneuvering, rather than with whole fabric blocks.

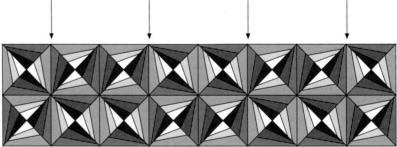

Pattern Ten, border possibility.

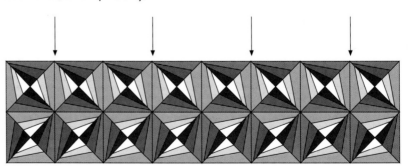

Border above with every other section between arrows turned upside-down.

Pattern Eleven
Herringbones vs. Vertical Stripes on a Diagonal Field

Note that when you squint at the A blocks in this arrangement, you see herringbone-type patterns; if you look at pairs of vertical rows, a "corn stalk" motif emerges. This same pattern in the B block, however, makes one set of vertical rows (the even-numbered ones) seem closer to the viewer, while the remaining rows show a pattern of light and dark diagonals.

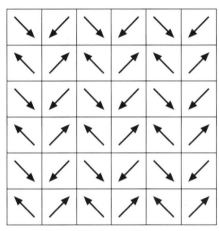

Pattern Eleven: Block Rotation

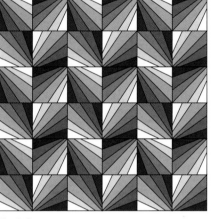

Block A

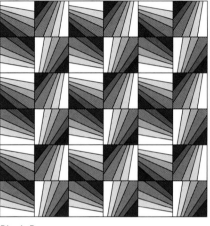

Block B

Since this pattern has such a vertical feeling to it, another maneuver to try is to cut it apart along horizontal lines to see what happens. Look how many different zigzag designs can be obtained this way. Perhaps these could be put together end-to-end as borders.

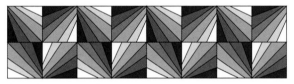

Rows 1 and 2, A Blocks

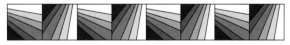

Row 1, A Blocks

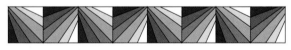

Rows 2 and 3, A Blocks

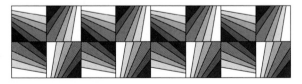

Rows 1 and 2, B Blocks

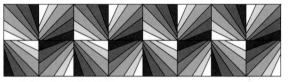

Row 1, B Blocks

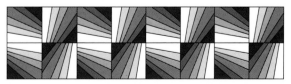

Rows 2 and 3, B Blocks

Pattern Eleven, cut apart along horizontal lines.

Pattern Twelve
A Linear Design

This pattern is very versatile because it is so directional and so linear. Note that in both the A and B blocks, a strong diagonal is formed.

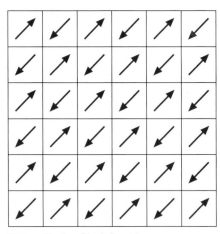

Pattern Twelve: Block Rotation

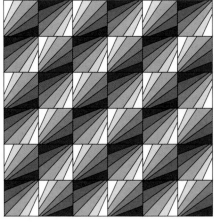

Block A

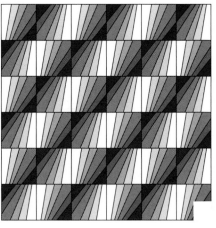

Block B

There are a number of motifs you could develop with such a design. The first of these would be to use the diagonal in two directions.

Block A

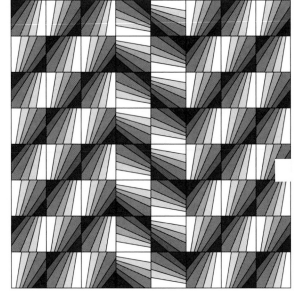

Block B

Pattern Twelve, diagonal in two directions.

If you use this pattern in all four directions, you could form a diamond motif; or the opposite, a radiating design.

Block A

Block B

Pattern Twelve, diamond motif.

Block A

Block B

Pattern Twelve, radiating design.

A variation on this theme would make these diagonals form a spiral. Note that there are multiple ways of resolving the beginning of the spiral, and that it need not begin "dead center" in the quilt.

The spiral idea was the springboard for my quilt *Comet*, pictured below.

Pattern Twelve, spiral design.

COMET

61" X 61"

Margaret J. Miller, 1997

Woodinville, Washington

The impetus for making this quilt was working with a spiral design from a linear pattern.

Yet another possibility with a linear design is to form a weaving pattern. Though it is possible to weave linear patterns right next to each other, it is a more readable design if a "spacer block" is used to separate the linear strands that are woven together.

Pattern Twelve, weaving pattern.

With spacer block

Doris Northcutt explored this weaving idea in her quilt *Fire and Ice*. Note that she allowed the woven strands to escape into the border, and used multiple single fabric blocks there to give them some "breathing space," thus bringing the quilt to an effective visual close.

FIRE AND ICE

72" X 72"

Doris Northcutt, 1997

Greenbank, Washington,

Note the single fabric (unpieced) squares in this quilt that give the weaving design "breathing room."

Blocks Arranged On Point

Since the Easy Pieces blocks are four-sided parallelograms, they can be used as squares or diamond shapes. Therefore, all of the above patterns could be considered as "on point" designs as well as arrangements of squares. In order to view the patterns previously considered, take a photocopy of any pattern on page 43, glue it to file folder tagboard, and cut out a "window" in the following configuration.

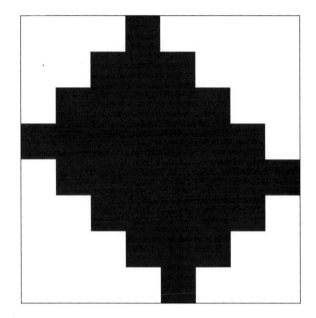

To view on point, cut out a window in this configuration.

When you turn the cardboard page over, you have a "window" through which to look at a complete quilt design of blocks on point. Merely turning the illustrations in the book so they are on point isn't very helpful. Since the blocks don't line up in rows as they would in a real quilt, it is hard to envision what the real pattern would be.

Place this window onto each of the photocopies of the patterns previously presented (see pages 27-45), and, to see the pattern more clearly, look through a reducing glass. Be sure to move your window around the design a little, because something that looks uninteresting may be a wonderful design when the window is shifted one block up or down, or one block to the right or left!

There is a danger in playing with only black-and-white line designs—you may discount the patterns that look very simple. Yet look what Callie Smith did with the simplest on-point block arrangement, Pattern One, in her magnificent quilt *Under the Sea* (pictured on page 86). It is important to have a set of real blocks on your design wall to work with at the same time you are playing with line design. The more blocks, the better. To have the most fun with designing, you should have at least twice the basic set of thirty-two blocks made with the instructions given on pages 11-22.

Be sure to try out interesting patterns you find on paper in A blocks, then in B blocks, and finally in B reversal blocks. The real fun, of course, is to combine different types of blocks (like B's and B Reversals, or A's and B's) on the design wall for each block-on-point pattern.

The same maneuvers applied to square blocks apply to arrangements of on-point blocks. For example, if you find a linear directional element, look for ways to use that element in at least two directions in your quilt, if not in four directions. My quilts *Polliwogs* (seen on page 9) and *Afternoon at the Zoo* (page 123) are very similar treatments of the linear Pattern Twelve, composed of A blocks and mirror image A blocks.

Two quilts that use B blocks in the same design are my *Seattle Summer—Still Raining* (page 105, 127), and Pat Johnston's quilt *Wedgitivity* (page 54). Pat's quilt shows directional patterns with A and B blocks on point.

When trying the patterns as squares and then as blocks on point, you may be surprised to see some patterns become more bold in one orientation than another. In my quilt *Labyrinth* (page 109), the zigzag border emerged when I took a photo of blocks arranged in Pattern Eight and turned the photo on point. The beginning of that quilt on the design wall, was the zigzag border; the rest of the quilt was an experiment in using the lightest wedge of a Block B to create line design.

Maggie Ball used Pattern Ten on point as her jumping off place for *Psychedelic Pinwheels* (see page 82), though this is well disguised by the fact that some motifs are from blocks, some are from mirror images, and some have separators while others do not.

In her quilt *Sassy Boxes*, Janice Maddox isolated two motifs from Pattern Ten. These motifs overlap in the pattern, but by separating and then checkerboarding them in her blocks-on-point arrangement, she created this stunning quilt. The roundness of the peach motifs behind the dark green diamonds is a lovely counterpoint, and the way the border triangles seem to shimmer as they advance and recede is delightful!

SASSY BOXES
54" X 68"
Janice Maddox, 1997
Asheville, North Carolina

The more you look at this quilt, the more you see in it: Note that the "blocks" are defined by the middle seam of the A block, not by a block edge seam!

Combining Blocks and Their Mirror Images

Adding the mirror image factor to arrangements of Easy Pieces blocks introduces a whole new world of quilt design possibilities. There are some designs that you can make symmetrical just by rotating the block, but there are others for which this is not possible unless you have mirror image blocks to work with.

The use of the mirror image block gives you more options in turning a design in the opposite direction. In the medallion quilts below, the examples on the left are created with only A blocks. On the right, the quilts are blocks in two quarters, and mirror image blocks in the opposite two.

Medallion quilt using only A blocks.

Medallion quilt using A blocks and mirror image A blocks.

Use of the mirror image blocks gives a depth and emphasis to different areas of block patterns that is not otherwise possible. Notice how three-dimensional Kathleen Loomis's quilt *Blue Ridge Mountains* appears.

This is such a simple pattern (Block B and mirror image B "checkerboarded" across the surface), yet Kathleen's careful placement of the few blocks with very dark values, as well as the blocks containing the yellow print fabric, gives the viewer ample reason to pause over this quilt.

Sally B. Davis also put lots of visual food for thought in her quilt *Reflection*. Though there are only A blocks in this quilt, the combination of blocks and their mirror images enabled Sally to play with horizontal vs. vertical diamonds, and use half-diamonds to help frame the central twenty-four blocks of this quilt.

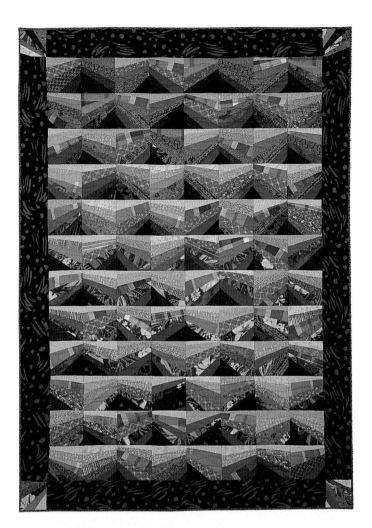

BLUE RIDGE MOUNTAINS

61" X 86"

Kathleen Loomis, 1997

Louisville, Kentucky

A simple block arrangement made dramatic by the placement of specific fabrics.

REFLECTION

53½" X 42"

Sally B. Davis, 1997

Warren, New Jersey

The diamond theme is echoed in the quilting, using new angles not present in the pieced work.

FOREST FRENZY

45" X 45"

Allyn Humphreys, 1997

Arlington, Virginia

Machine quilted by Margaret J. Miller.
When you squint at this quilt, the pinwheels in the center begin to dance!

Sprinkling mirror image motifs throughout your quilt surface gives a refreshing look to a repeat pattern. Allyn Humphreys's quilt *Forest Frenzy* is a good example of this. Note that she used Pattern Ten, but each group of four blocks alternates with a group of four mirror image blocks in the same pattern. When you squint your eyes at her quilt, look at how she has created the effect of "dancing pinwheels." Each pinwheel spins a different direction from its neighbors.

In her quilt *The Inside Story*, Nancy Meyer also sprinkled blocks and their mirror images in an interesting way. Pattern Ten sets off the panel print in an unusual way because of the role played by the striped fabric in every block. One of the delights of this quilt is the continuation of the panel figure into the dark triangle in the block below it. It looks like the ladies are stepping out of the patchwork quilt! Note also how Nancy used blocks as the bottom border, mirror image blocks for the top border, and a combination of both for the sides. The absence of the striped fabric makes for quite an effective border.

THE INSIDE STORY

44½" X 55¾"

Nancy Meyer, 1997

Spring Lake, Michigan

The dark fabric in one of the blocks of this quilt joins with the dark leg of one of the figures, so it appears that she is stepping out of this quilt!

LIGHT SETS IN

41" X 41"

A. Jean Coppola, 1997

Shoreham, New York

Even the simplest patterns can be dramatic in Easy Pieces quilts.

Jean Coppola combined blocks, mirror images, and patterns in her quilt *Light Sets In*. The longer you look at this quilt, the more you see in it. Even though the "X" pattern is fairly consistent, the diamond groupings are all slightly different from each other because of the direction of the blocks which form them. Note that this quilt seems to have two distinct sets of blocks. This is the result when you flip and sew all the wedges without varying the fabric combinations by occasionally moving wedge pairs to the bottom of their same-width pile.

creating quilts with easy pieces blocks

A very effective block/mirror image border was created by Phyllis Thompson in her quilt *Japanese Lanterns*. Note the rounded feeling she achieved by including one yellow block in each of the orange corner motifs.

Always keep in mind that these patterns are only jumping off places to quilt design. One way the patterns can be used is to pull out selected motifs from them, and let the design transform as the eye scans the quilt. Marty Kutz did this in her quilt *He Is Risen*, which is one of a series of quilts she has made for her church community. Note how she changed the direction of the diamond motifs through the creation of the cross and how the rest of the blocks form a light-filled background to that motif.

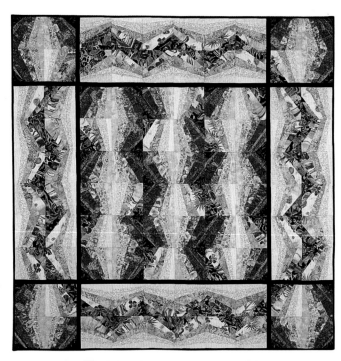

JAPANESE LANTERNS

56" X 56"

Phyllis Thompson, 1997

Leola, Pennsylvania

This quilt is a good example of the drama of block/mirror image block combinations.

HE IS RISEN

44" X 55"

Marty Kutz, 1995

Sedro Woolley, Washington

One of a series of quilts Marty has made for her church community; this was for the Easter season.

Combining Blocks A and B

All the preceding arrangements can be created using both A and B blocks. To help you wade through the hundreds of other ways these blocks can go together, here are a few simple approaches to get you started!

Start with your favorite arrangement of A blocks. When you place the B blocks on the wall according to the following suggestions, make sure they are oriented the same way as the A block they replaced.

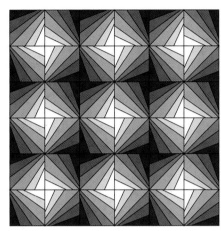

Pattern with A Blocks

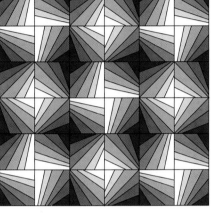

Right

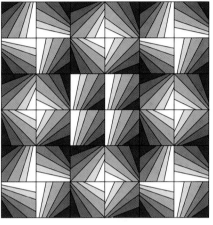

Wrong

1. Replace every other block with Block B.
2. Checkerboard four A blocks, four B blocks over the entire surface. (This is the example shown above.)
3. Replace the center four blocks with B blocks. Replace the outermost row (on all four sides) with B blocks. If there is space in the quilt, replace another row between the center and the border row with B blocks.
4. Replace alternate vertical (or horizontal) rows with B blocks.
5. In a pattern with regularly repeated motifs, replace:

    a) every other motif with B blocks;

    b) every other row of motifs with the same motif expressed in B blocks; or

    c) an A block motif only every so often over the surface of the quilt with that motif in B blocks.

WEDGETIVITY

54" X 54"

Patricia R. Johnston, 1997

Brookings, Oregon

Brilliant combination of A blocks
and B blocks, all in the same color
palette.

QUILTED TABLE RUNNERS

19½" X 52" AND 14¾" X 47"

Evie Newall, 1995

Seattle, Washington

One to keep, one to give away!
Good use of a focus fabric in the
middle of the block.

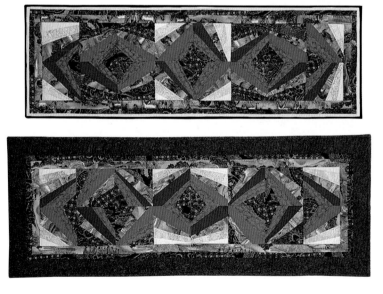

Pat Johnston combined A and B blocks magnificently in her quilt *Wedgetivity*. Note that the area of the quilt where the B blocks reside seems to be a more quiet design area in the quilt: the patterns formed by the A blocks tend to dominate.

Evie Newall also used both A and B blocks in making her table runners. The subtle change in the shape of the diamonds formed by the gold wedges is the type of detail that makes a quilt interesting to look at, because you can't look at only one small portion of the quilt and predict accurately what the rest of the quilt will look like!

Combining A and B blocks does not always result in dramatic line design changes in the patterns, since the difference between the two blocks is a change in the angle of the seams within the block. Adding B blocks to a pattern that is made up primarily of A blocks adds more light to the entire design, because of the first two light wedges of the B block.

Combining Block B and Block B Reversals

Since Block B is an asymmetrical block, it is possible to combine it with its reverse version in the arrangements already discussed. Regular Block B goes light to dark, wedge to triangle, while "Reverse B" goes dark to light. The reverse B block also has a mirror image.

Block B

Block B
Mirror Image

Reverse Block B

Reverse Block B
Mirror Image

For dramatic change in a given pattern, add reverse B block to your mix of blocks! Using reverse B adds a weight and richness to the overall pattern, because it adds dark and medium-dark values to the design.

As you play with photocopies of various patterns, sometimes you get some interesting surprises. Look what happened when Pattern Three was created using reverse B blocks—the rows of blocks no longer look parallel!

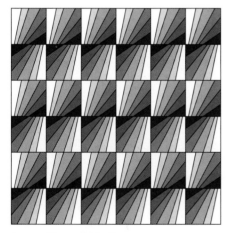 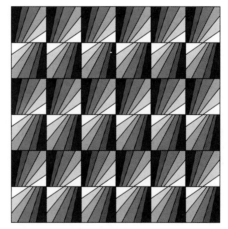

Pattern Three, B blocks

Reverse B blocks

There are striking differences in the look of reverse B block patterns depending on where you start or stop your pattern. Again, a very regular block arrangement transforms into a design that appears slightly off kilter.

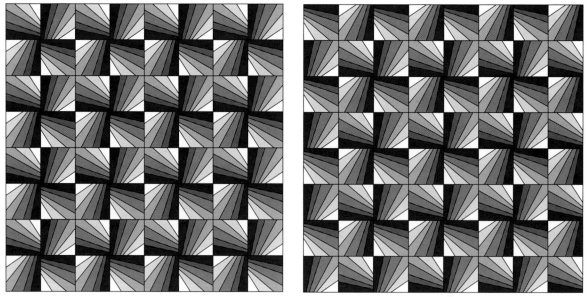

Some reverse B block patterns appear slightly off kilter.

Combining regular B blocks with reverse B blocks can transform a pattern into a more exciting design than can be made with either of these blocks used alone. In the example below, groups of four regular blocks were "checkerboarded" over the pattern formed with reverse B blocks. Note how the dark pinwheel was simplified, and how it reaches into neighboring blocks. When you squint at this pattern or look at it through a reducing glass, sometimes the dark pinwheels are more obvious, sometimes the light ones.

Combining regular B Blocks with reverse B blocks can transform a pattern.

You may wish to play with photocopies of designs first or go directly to the blocks. If you go directly to the blocks, go through all the patterns on pages 27-42, placing the B blocks in each arrangement in turn, and placing the reverse B blocks in the same pattern to the right of them. Take photographs of each arrangement.

Before leaving each pattern to go to the next, try substituting some reverse B blocks for regular blocks, following the shaded diagrams below. (Note: Put all your blocks onto the wall in whatever configuration you choose, even though the number of squares in the diagram may differ from the number of blocks you have on hand.) Let the shaded square represent the reverse B block (the light ones are the regular B blocks). In this process, first substitute the reverse B blocks on the design wall in an upright position. When they are all in place, look at the arrangement through a reducing glass to decide how you are going to rotate them in place to create a pleasing quilt pattern.

Design grids

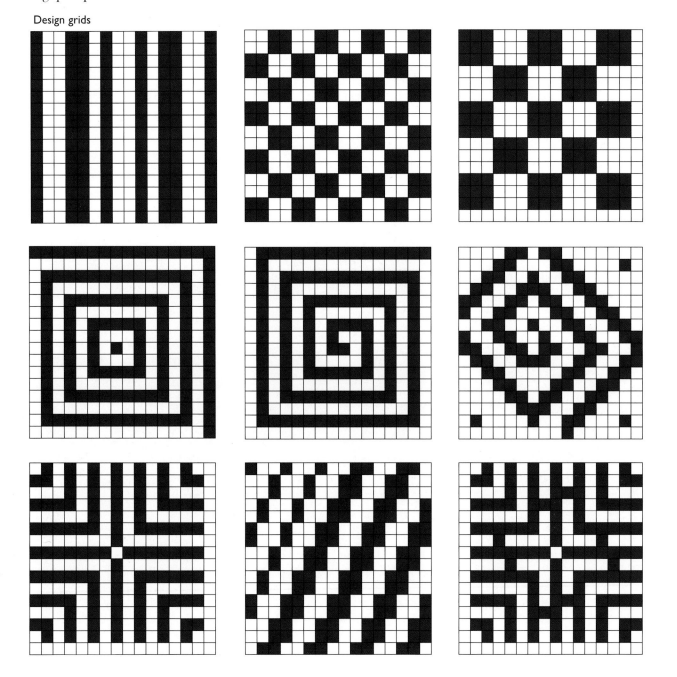

Design grids

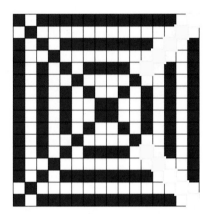
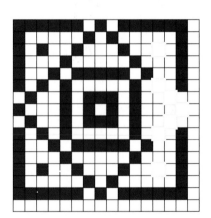
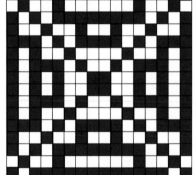
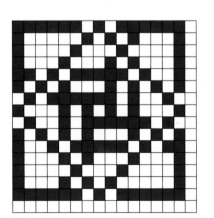
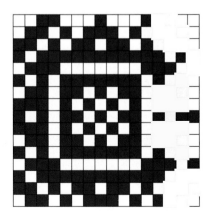

Because the reverse B block significantly changes the look of the quilt due to the amount of medium to dark values it adds, there are more possibilities for mixing it with either regular B blocks or regular A blocks. The illustrations below show step-by-step how reverse B blocks dramatically change the look of a quilt in place on your design wall.

Reverse B blocks can dramatically change the look of a quilt.

A, B, and A-B Mirror Images

Reverse B Blocks substituted

Reverse B Blocks rotated to match positioning in original quilt above.

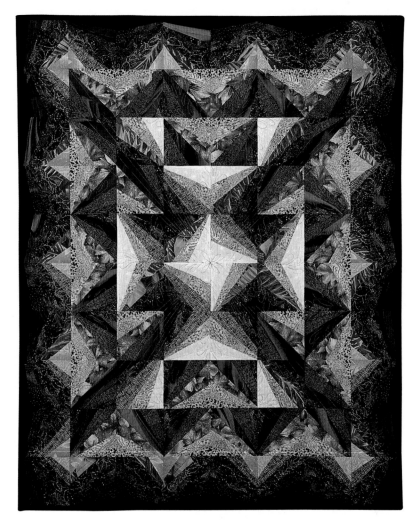

FALL FROST

46" X 56"

Marty Kutz, 1997

Sedro Woolley, Washington

High contrast provides the drama in this quilt; note how effectively reverse B blocks were used to form a border for this quilt.

A good example of what reverse B blocks add to the quilt is Marty Kutz's quilt *Fall Frost*. The border blocks in this quilt are all reverse B blocks. Note how the lights appear sharper in the center of the quilt, and the scalloped inner border formed by the light shapes in the border blocks.

USING *ALL* THE BLOCKS…YES, IT IS POSSIBLE

You will probably start with a design strategy and try to pursue it in an organized fashion. Before you know it, you will be juggling blocks furiously as inspiration hits, and "plugging them in" on your design wall with wild abandon. It is very helpful to keep your blocks in separate piles near your design wall for easy access. Keep each type of block in its own pile (A's, A Mirrors; B's, B Mirrors; Reverse B's, Reverse B Mirrors). If you are using more than one color family, you will have that many more rows of piles of blocks. I find setting up a spare ironing board perpendicular to the design wall is useful for this purpose. It can also hold my camera and my idea book as well.

In her quilt *Wedgies*, Carol Blevins used Pattern Eleven (viewed sideways) as her jumping off place, but look how that simple pattern transformed as she used A and B blocks in one row, their mirror images in the next, etc.

WEDGIES

53½" X 64"

Carol Blevins, 1996

Red Lion, Pennsylvania

Good example of making a subtle pattern transformation by using A and B blocks as well as their mirror images.

Below is the plan for a medallion quilt that also uses all the types of blocks we have discussed so far. Before tackling a quilt like this using real blocks (rather than black/white photocopy design), set up a system ahead of time that keeps your blocks organized—it will save you a lot of time in the long run.

Quilt design using all the block possibilities.

OFFSETTING BLOCKS

We have already touched on this possibility on page 32 when we offset the round motifs of Patterns Six and Seven, thus forming a zigzag pattern between motifs. However, you can also produce new designs by offsetting rows of blocks from each other in an organized manner. For example, you can offset rows of blocks horizontally or vertically; by a whole or a half block; in only one direction, or more than one.

Offsetting by a Whole Block

Begin by arranging your blocks on the wall in one of the patterns described above.

Take horizontal Row Two, and move it to the right by one block. Leave Row Three in place, and move Row Four to the right in the same manner.

Take the block on the right that sticks out and put it in the hole on the left created by shifting the row.

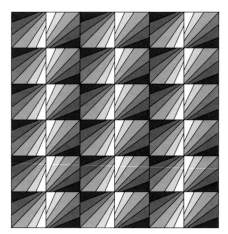

Pattern design

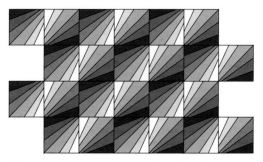

Offset the even rows one block to the right.

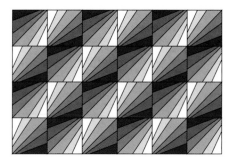

Move the blocks that stick out to fill the holes.

In some arrangements, this offsetting makes a difference in the pattern; in others it makes none. Now take Row Four and put it back in its original position, then move it to the left by one block. With some patterns, the shift to the right produces a different pattern than does a shift to the left.

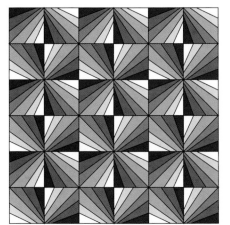

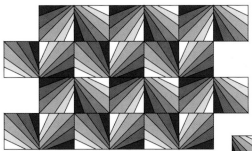

Offset the even rows one block to the left.

Pattern design

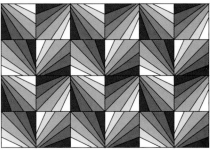

Move the blocks that stick out to fill the holes.

Now put the blocks back into the original arrangement (the one you had before any rows were moved). Take the second vertical row and move it down by one block; take the fourth vertical row and move it up by one block. Again, your choices are to offset the rows of blocks by one block either in the same direction or in opposite directions.

Pattern design

Shift one row down by one block, shift one up by one block.

Move the blocks that stick out to fill the holes.

Remember that the fun of designing an Easy Pieces quilt is not to choose only one pattern, but to begin the quilt with one pattern, and transform it into another as the eye travels over the surface of the quilt. This transformation might be as simple as interrupting the pattern in part of the quilt with an offset version of the pattern.

Interrupt part of the pattern with an offset version.

Offsetting by a Half-block

Much more exciting possibilities emerge when you offset rows by a half-block. Make an arrangement on the wall. Following the diagrams below, move selected rows one-half block to the right or left.

Step back and take a look (and maybe a photograph!).

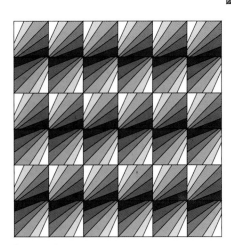

Pattern design

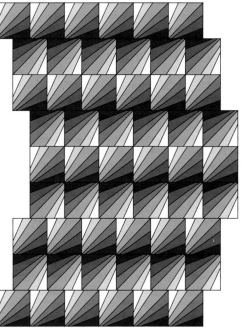

Single and paired rows offset from each other.

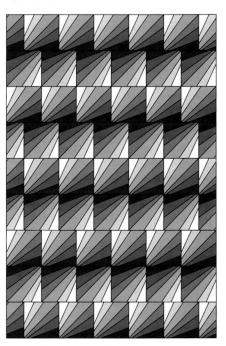

Rows trimmed and sides even; squint and notice the different types of white shapes.

Before moving on to another pattern, line the blocks up in their original position. Then move the vertical rows up or down by a half-block. Sometimes a different pattern emerges when rows are shifted one direction than when they are shifted the other direction.

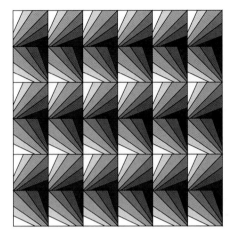

Pattern design

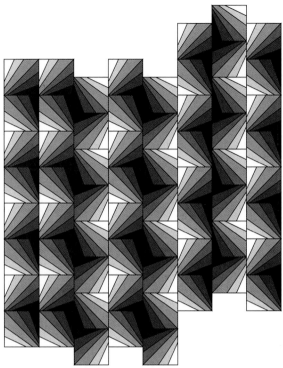

Blocks offset by a half-block in two different directions.

One half-block shift produces spool shapes; the other produces a "barbed wire" motif.

Try these maneuvers with several of the patterns given on pages 27-43.

This approach may seem to pose some piecing problems, because of the partial block shapes needed to complete the row. The most efficient way to handle this is to sew a whole block to the end of the row; once the rows are all sewn together, true up the four sides with an acrylic ruler and a rotary cutter. (See illustration on page 69.)

LIGHTS ON MY
CHRISTMAS TREE
67" x 67"

Maurine Roy, 1996

Edmonds, Washington

A good example of using blocks off-set from each other; note also the border within a border was made from segments of B blocks sewn end to end.

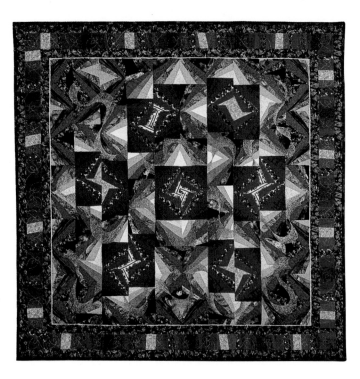

Maurine Roy combined offset rows with matching rows of blocks in her quilt *Lights on My Christmas Tree*. Note the variation she achieved in the light center areas of the red blocks; they truly look like Christmas lights sparkling through tree branches!

In Grace Crocker's quilt called *Quilt Virus* we see how subtly you can change the angle of a design motif by offsetting blocks. In traditional patchwork, we have the choice of making designs move horizontally, vertically, or at a 45-degree angle. By offsetting B blocks particularly, you can create some very subtle angles and even the suggestion of strong curves (seen in the upper-right and lower-left branches of Grace's crossed motif lines).

QUILT VIRUS
75" X 57"

Grace M. Crocker, 1996

Glenn, California

Good example of using offset blocks to form very subtle curves.

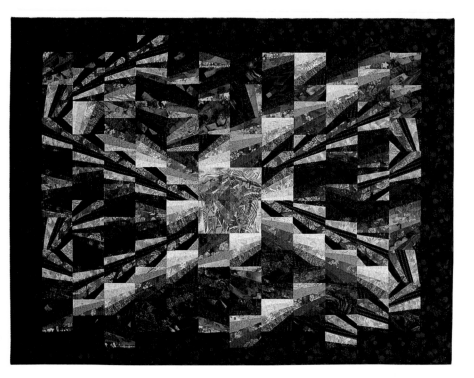

COSMOS
47" X 64"
Carole A. Liebzeit, 1994
Cincinnati, Ohio

An example of offsetting both horizontally and vertically in the same quilt! Note that the compensating spacer blocks were used sometimes boldly, sometimes with subtlety.

Carole Liebzeit offset her blocks by a partial block *both* horizontally *and* vertically in her quilt *Cosmos*. Note the narrow rectangles she used as spacers. Sometimes these blend right into the row of blocks; in other places they stand out as accents. Notice how offsetting the rows enabled her to let the quilt "invade" the border in a couple of places, and how effective a border technique this is.

Now that your eyes are thoroughly crossed, it is time to cut you loose to play with your own blocks! Obviously, the best starting point is to choose only one of the directions laid out in this chapter as your jumping off place (all A blocks; or, A's and their mirror images; or, A's and B's; etc.). Regardless of your approach, before you settle on a final design, try these strategies on your design wall:

1. Directional pattern? Use at least two ways, if not four.
2. Linear pattern? Try making a concentric (such as Barn Raising) design with it, or perhaps a spiral. Don't forget to try to make it weave in certain areas of the design.
3. Regular repeat motif? Try offsetting all or some of them.
4. Try combining whole motifs and partial (half and quarter) motifs.
5. Take the top row, put it on the bottom.
6. Take the side row, put it on the other side.
7. Offset the rows—by a whole block, by a half block; both horizontally and vertically.
8. Substitute mirror image blocks in selected areas of the pattern.
9. Substitute reverse B blocks in certain areas of the pattern.
10. Purposely incorporate more than one pattern in your design.
11. Purposely make your pattern transpose (through offsetting, perhaps) as the eye travels across the quilt surface.

Most important of all, have fun playing with these arrangements, and KEEP A CAMERA HANDY, as well as your idea book to jot down your inspirations as they occur!

SEWING THE BLOCKS TOGETHER

Sewing Easy Pieces quilts together is simple. You have only square shapes to sew together.

Some people sew rows together first, and press the seam allowances between blocks in alternate directions from row to row. Thus when the rows are sewn together, the seam allowances lock together, ensuring an accurate joining.

I prefer to press the seams between blocks open to distribute the bulk more evenly. I am also in the habit of pressing the seams that join rows open, rather than to one side.

When making quilts in which the blocks are offset from one another, first I sew rows of blocks together. Then when it is time to join rows, I fold a few blocks in one row in half to determine the center of the block, and mark it with a straight pin. Then I have a specific place to match the seam from the next row. By pin marking and matching in this manner several times along a row, your offset blocks will be sewn together more accurately.

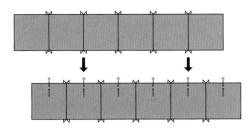

Match the seamlines of one row with the midpoints of the blocks in the next row which have been marked with pins.

In offset arrangements, I make whole blocks for the odd spaces left over at the end of the row. Once all the rows are sewn together, I trim the excess block sections off using a rotary cutter and acrylic ruler. If the quilt is very large, I use two large carpenter's T-squares in the corners to make sure I am trimming accurately.

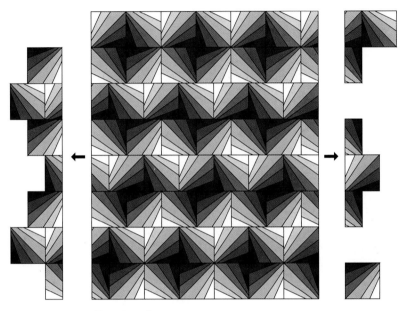

Trim the edges even.

Most importantly, stay-stitch all edges of your quilt as soon as it is sewn together even if you are going to layer, baste, and quilt it immediately! Remember that ALL the blocks have bias edges (only the B block has one straight-grain edge!), so distortion of the edges of your quilt is likely unless you do a line of stitching all around the quilt, about ¼" in from the edge.

color, color, and more color

the best thing Easy Pieces teaches is the blending of fabrics, colors, and values. You may wish to begin by exploring one color family only, and become proficient in utilizing a full range of value with your early sets of Easy Pieces blocks.

In her quilt *Diamonds and Sapphires*, Avis Caddell used this approach, following a long-term desire to express the iciness of blues in a full range of values. Her use of lamé and satin and other shiny fabrics is most effective, complemented by her machine quilting with a metallic silver thread.

DIAMONDS AND SAPPHIRES

36" X 36"

Avis B. Caddell, 1995

Sidney, British Columbia, Canada

This quilt has silks, satins, lamés, and cottons; the quilting with highly reflective metallic thread adds even more shimmer. Finished blocks are only four inches in size.

UNDERSEA BLUEGREENS
48" X 48"

Flo Peel, 1997

Qualicum Beach,

British Columbia, Canada

Even before the leaves were appliquéd onto this quilt, it was a brilliant study in value within one color family. The leaves appear to be floating on the water.

Flo Peel also began by staying in one color family in her quilt *Undersea Bluegreens*. Though she added another color family with the appliquéd leaves, note that she thoroughly explored a full range of values in blue-greens, using contrast of the darkest blocks among the lighter ones to create movement.

Once you have played with Easy Pieces blocks for a while, and get a feeling for spreading value over the quilt surface, you may wish to add additional color families to these blocks for even more excitement. In this chapter you will see a number of ways to accomplish this. Begin with your basic set of blocks, and add to them as you go along.

MAKE ANOTHER SET OF BLOCKS

The simplest approach is to make another set of blocks in another color family. If your basic set of blocks were blue blocks with a touch of red, maybe you will make all gold blocks with accents of orange for your second set.

Or, perhaps you would make new sets of blocks for this experiment; one set of yellow-orange blocks, another set of blue-purple blocks. The number of actual fabrics you use for each set is up to you. You might use the same number of fabrics (six or twelve) in each color family, or use only six fabrics in the yellow-orange set and twelve fabrics in the blue-purple one.

Begin by putting your blocks in place on the design wall without paying attention to the actual pattern they form (put them all up oriented the same direction, if you wish). Start by "checkerboarding" the blocks from the two color families.

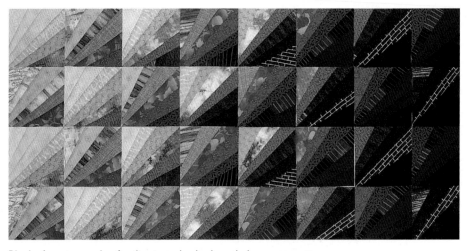

Blocks from two color families in a checkerboarded arrangement.
Note how strong the blending is.

There are many other ways of placing blocks from two or more color families onto your design wall. Refer to the shaded diagrams on pages 57-58 for a number of ways to combine color families; the white squares represent blocks from one color family, the shaded squares represent the blocks of the other color family. (Note: The number of squares illustrated may differ from the number of blocks you made—put all your blocks onto the wall in whatever configuration you choose.)

Without taking the blocks down from the wall, rotate them in place and see what some of the patterns from pages 27-45 look like with this new larger group of blocks. Again, keep a camera handy—you may stumble onto some wonderful quilt possibilities along the way!

Once you have played with blocks made from two color families for a while, introducing a set of blocks from a third and even a fourth color family would be interesting. See Appendix A (page 132) for a brief summary of Johannes Itten's system for playing with a color wheel to select multiple color families. I use this system often, not only to select colors I enjoy working with, but also to select fabric colors I have never worked with before.

ADDING COLOR ONE WEDGE AT A TIME

After you have played with blocks made from two color families, consider making a transitional set of blocks. In this set, the second color family is introduced one shape at a time; the second color starts to take over the first one. This set of blocks often softens areas of a quilt where you don't want the strong contrast of two color families against each other. Transition blocks are more effective if you have multiples of each type.

With this approach you will use a slightly different procedure for cutting and laying out triangles and wedges. Let's assume you have eight red fabrics and eight purple ones, and that you are cutting 6" A blocks. First, lay out each color family lighter toward darker. In each color family you will need triangles of the lightest and the darkest fabrics; and triangles and wedges of all other fabrics in between.

To Cut Triangles

Stack four fabrics from the run so the selvages and folds are parallel. Crosscut 5½" as on page 11.

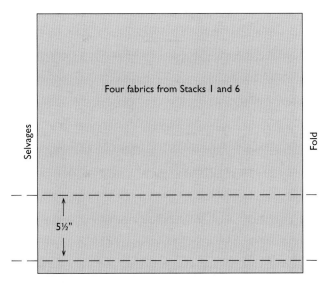

Stack four fabrics from Stacks 1 and 6 and crosscut 5½".

Then, working with only one fabric at a time, take the 5½" crosscut and fold it in half. Align the cut edges and selvages and trim off the selvages with a rotary cutter.

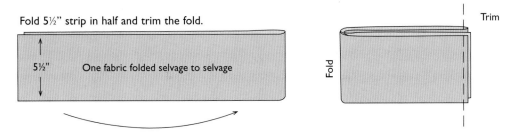

From this folded 5½" strip, starting at the cut end (not the folded end), subcut two 4" rectangles. Unfold the end of the 5½" strip and cut one more 4" subcut.

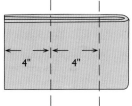

Subcut 4" rectangles.

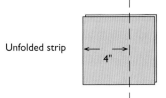

Unfold remaining section and subcut 4".

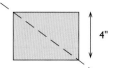

Stacked rectangles cut
corner to corner.

Stack the rectangles and cut corner to corner. If your rotary cutter isn't very sharp, you may have to make a couple stacks to cut! Stack all triangles of the same fabric in one pile. Repeat for the other three fabrics to be cut into triangles.

To Cut Wedges

Stack four fabrics beginning with fabric number 2 with the folds and selvages aligned. It doesn't matter which fabrics you choose, since all wedges will be separated by fabric eventually. Crosscut 9" as on page 13.

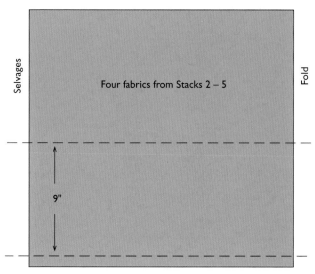

Stack four fabrics and crosscut 9".

Then, *working with only one fabric at a time*, fold the 9" strip in half, and trim off the selvages and fold with a single cut.

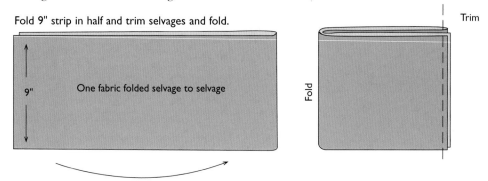

From this folded 9" strip, starting at the cut end (not the folded end), subcut one 3½" strip and one 3" strip. Unfold the remaining 9" strip and cut one more 3½" subcut and one more 3" subcut.

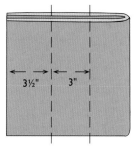

Subcut 3½" and 3".

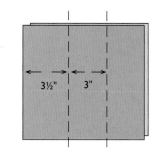

Unfold strip and subcut 3½" and 3".

Stack matching subcuts together and cut at an angle to create the wedges. Keep the narrower wedges together, and the wider wedges together; stack in a staggered fashion with the straight grain on the left.

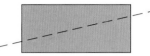

Cut wedges from rectangles.

Instead of chain piecing the piles of wedges and triangles, you will be assembling one block at a time. For Blocks A or B, lay out the triangles and wedges as you did for the original set of blocks; lights on the left toward darks on the right. Remember to alternate wides and narrows in succeeding piles of wedges.

With your yellow-oranges and blue-purples cut and laid out within easy reach of the sewing machine, make at least two blocks of each type in the transition series. Make two blocks that are made of five yellow-orange shapes and one blue-purple one; the next pair would have four yellow-orange shapes and two blue-purple ones, etc. Eventually you will have a block with all yellow-oranges.

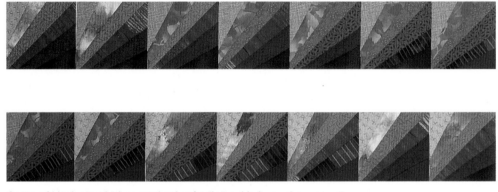

Series of blocks in which second color family is added one shape at a time.

When you have made the transition to the other color family (blue-purples), you may begin adding yellow-oranges again one shape at a time. Or, you might introduce an entirely different color family at this point. With this process you would have a third color family in the quilt that would act as an accent color, since there would always be more blocks of the original two color families. Adding color families one shape at a time builds subtlety in color flow in your quilt.

USING A RUN OF FABRICS

Another approach to spreading color across the quilt surface is to start with many colors rather than one or two. Go to your fabric collection and select a "run" of fabrics; maybe light to dark in one color family, maybe around the color wheel, from yellows to greens to blues (warm colors to cool colors). Any number of values may be used. Start with ten to fifteen fabrics. You will need at least one-half yard of each of the fabrics you choose.

To begin my quilt *Sunrise, Sunset*, I began with a range of warm colors, from yellows to oranges to reds to browns. There were sixteen fabrics on my swatch sheet, and I began by making three blocks of fabrics one through six, three more blocks of fabrics two through seven, three more of fabrics three through eight, and so on until I had reached the end of the swatch sheet. I made another run of blocks for the border, with a few extra of the very lightest and very darkest ones for more emphasis.

SUNRISE, SUNSET

38" X 49½"

Margaret J. Miller, 1996

Woodinville, Washington

An example of working with a series of sixteen fabrics, taken in order, from a swatch sheet.

COMPLEMENTS OF THE
SEASON
45" X 67"
Avis B. Caddell, 1995
Sidney, British Columbia, Canada

Avis made this quilt to be photographed and used as her Christmas card. She received a few cards in reply which gently tried to correct her spelling of the word "complement" . . . from those who didn't understand the play on words!

In her quilt *Complements of the Season*, Avis Caddell went to her fabric cupboard and pulled out all her Christmasy fabrics. Note how masterfully she not only went from green to red (complementary colors), but blended her fabrics for a smooth transition from dark to light to dark again.

Remember that it is easier to see fabrics in relation to each other if you stagger them along a table or floor in such a way that you can see only about two inches of each fabric. Squint your eyes, or look at the run of fabrics through a reducing glass, and you will be able to see value more, and color less.

Most importantly, do this process as quickly as you can, and *do not agonize* over placement of specific fabrics in this run. If you are debating the position of two adjacent fabrics, this means they are probably interchangeable; so leave them in whatever position is more appealing to you, and move on.

Make a swatch sheet of these fabrics, placing the swatches in the order you have selected. Place the number one next to the first swatch on the swatch sheet, and increase the numbers as you go down the sheet—the largest number will be placed next to the last fabric in the run.

Sample swatch sheet

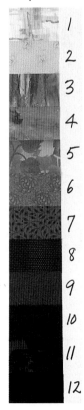

You will be organizing, cutting, and sewing your blocks differently when you work with a run of fabrics. If you are working with Block A, for example, and you have ten fabrics in the run, you will need triangles of more than only the lightest and darkest values. Any one block will have only six fabrics in it, but to take advantage of a subtle movement along the run of fabrics you have selected, you will be making the following blocks.

Note that you need triangles of all the fabrics in the run, and that you need more wedges of some fabrics than others.

Fabric	1	2	3	4	5	6	7	8	9	10
Block 1	T	W	W	W	W	T				
Block 2		T	W	W	W	W	T			
Block 3			T	W	W	W	W	T		
Block 4				T	W	W	W	W	T	
Block 5					T	W	W	W	W	T

T = Triangles W = Wedges

If you were making Block B from a run of ten fabrics, you would need the following wedges and triangles. For Block B, you would need triangles and wedges of only values six through ten. You would need all wedges (no triangles) from values one through five.

Fabric	1	2	3	4	5	6	7	8	9	10
Block 1	W	W	W	W	W	T				
Block 2		W	W	W	W	W	T			
Block 3			W	W	W	W	W	T		
Block 4				W	W	W	W	W	T	
Block 5					W	W	W	W	W	T

A run of ten fabrics will yield five different kinds of blocks. (In general, subtract five from the total number of fabrics you have in your run, and that will be the number of different blocks that run will create.)

There are many *many* ways of sprinkling this run across the quilt surface. Just a few of these possibilities appear on page 79. In the diagram, the number one represents the block that starts with fabric number one of the swatch sheet, number two is the block that begins with fabric number two, etc.

Light (top) to Dark

1	1	1	1	1	1	1	1
2	2	2	2	2	2	2	2
3	3	3	3	3	3	3	3
4	4	4	4	4	4	4	3
5	5	5	5	5	5	5	5
6	6	6	6	6	6	6	6
7	7	7	7	7	7	7	7
8	8	8	8	8	8	8	8

Layers of Light

1	1	1	1	1	1	1	1
2	2	2	2	2	2	2	2
3	3	3	3	3	3	3	3
4	4	4	4	4	4	4	3
1	1	1	1	1	1	1	1
2	2	2	2	2	2	2	2
3	3	3	3	3	3	3	3
4	4	4	4	4	4	4	4

Diagonal Shaft of Light

1	2	3	4	5	6	7	8
2	1	2	3	4	5	6	7
3	2	1	2	3	4	5	6
4	3	2	1	2	3	4	5
5	4	3	2	1	2	3	4
6	5	4	3	2	1	2	3
7	6	5	4	3	2	1	2
8	7	6	5	4	3	2	1

Crossed Shafts of Light

1	2	3	4	5	4	3	2	1
2	1	2	3	4	3	2	1	2
3	2	1	2	3	2	1	2	3
4	3	2	1	2	1	2	3	4
5	4	3	2	1	2	3	4	5
4	3	2	1	2	1	2	3	4
3	2	1	2	3	2	1	2	3
2	1	2	3	4	3	2	1	2
1	2	3	4	5	4	3	2	1

Center Spotlight

4	4	4	4	4	4	4	4
4	3	3	3	3	3	3	4
4	3	2	2	2	2	3	4
4	3	2	1	1	2	3	4
4	3	2	1	1	2	5	4
4	3	2	2	2	2	3	4
4	3	3	3	3	3	3	4
4	4	4	4	4	4	4	4

Variation on Center Spotlight

7	8	7	8	7	8	7	8
8	5	6	5	6	5	6	7
7	6	3	4	3	4	5	8
8	5	4	1	2	3	6	7
7	6	3	2	1	4	5	8
8	5	4	3	4	3	6	7
7	6	5	6	5	6	5	8
8	7	8	7	8	7	8	7

Log Cabin

13	10	10	10	10	10	11
13	9	6	6	6	7	11
13	9	5	2	3	7	11
13	9	5	1	3	7	11
13	9	5	4	4	7	11
13	9	8	8	8	8	11
13	12	12	12	12	12	12

Variation on Log Cabin

7	6	6	6	6	6	11
7	5	4	4	4	9	11
7	5	3	2	7	9	11
7	5	3	1	7	9	11
7	5	3	8	8	9	11
7	5	10	10	10	10	11
7	12	12	12	12	12	12

Trip Around the World

7	6	5	4	5	6	7
6	5	4	3	4	5	6
5	4	3	2	3	4	5
4	3	2	1	2	3	4
5	4	3	2	3	4	5
6	5	4	3	4	5	6
7	6	5	4	5	6	7

Checkerboard

1	2	3	4	5	6	7	8
2	1	4	3	6	5	8	7
7	8	1	2	3	4	5	6
8	7	2	1	4	3	6	5
5	6	7	8	1	2	3	4
6	5	8	7	2	1	4	3
3	4	5	6	7	8	1	2
4	3	6	5	8	7	2	1

Checkerboard

1	(8)	2	(7)	3	(6)	4	(5)	5
(7)	1	(8)	2	(7)	3	(6)	4	(5)
2	(7)	1	(8)	2	(7)	3	(6)	4
(6)	2	(7)	1	(8)	2	(7)	3	(6)
3	(6)	2	(7)	1	(8)	2	(7)	3
(5)	3	(6)	2	(7)	1	(8)	2	(7)
4	(5)	3	(6)	2	(7)	1	(8)	2
(4)	4	(5)	3	(6)	2	(7)	1	(8)
5	(4)	4	(5)	3	(6)	2	(7)	1

Plain Number =	One Color Family
Circled Number =	Another Color Family

This number system can be used to represent other kinds of Easy Pieces blocks. For other ways to use numbers to plan quilts, see page 98.

Before cutting out wedges and triangles, it is a good idea to calculate how many of each type of block you need to complete the design you have chosen. To do this, count how many times each number appears in your diagram, and make a list that tells you how many of each type block you need for that design. An example below shows how simple this is to do.

Calculating number of blocks and block type needed.

Block Type	Blocks Needed
1	6
①	2
2	4
②	4
3	6
③	2
4	6
④	2
5	4
⑤	4
6	6
⑥	2
7	6
⑦	2
8	4
⑧	4

1	②	3	4	⑤	6	7	⑧
⑧	1	2	③	4	5	⑥	7
7	8	①	2	3	④	5	6
6	⑦	8	1	②	3	4	⑤
⑤	6	7	⑧	1	2	③	4
4	5	⑥	7	8	①	2	3
3	④	5	6	⑦	8	1	②
②	3	4	⑤	6	7	⑧	1

Plain Number	=	One Color Family
Circled Number	=	Another Color Family

You have probably learned by now that making Easy Pieces blocks is so simple to do that you are better off making too many blocks than too few; having blocks at hand gives you more flexibility as the design process continues. Having more blocks on the design wall rather than fewer is important when working with these blocks.

When using a run of fabrics, I cut triangles and wedges of almost all the fabrics in the run. If I know I am using only Block A, I cut triangles only of the very first and very last fabric in the run. If I know I am using only Block B, I cut wedges only of the first five fabrics in the run, triangles of only the last fabric, and triangles and wedges of the rest. To cut for such a run, I use the same cutting procedure described on page 72-75, in the section Adding Color One Wedge at a Time.

It is helpful to place this run of triangles and wedges on a surface close to your sewing machine (I use a spare ironing board) so you can pick up triangles and wedges as you need them. When working with a run of fabrics, I will make each block completely as needed, rather than doing the chain sewing as described in the basic directions, page 17. With this method, you can make only the particular blocks you think you will need for a given arrangement.

An alternative approach to working with a numbered diagram that represents the final quilt would be to start with a set number of each of the different types of blocks in the run, and build the quilt from there. For the quilt *Sunrise, Sunset* (on page 76), I made three of each type of block in the run (an arbitrary decision). As the blocks were made, I placed them on the wall. I purposely made each horizontal row only five blocks long—the quilt would have looked too predictable if the whole first row was block number one, the whole second row was block number two, etc. Better blending of the values and colors was achieved by having only three of each type of block.

Once the blocks for the body of the quilt were in place on the wall, planning the border began on graph paper, using numbers to represent the blocks. Since the quilt progresses from light at the top to dark at the bottom, the row of border blocks was planned to have the reverse light pattern—dark at one upper corner to light at the lower opposite corner.

Notice in the numbered drawing that I had to make more very light and more very dark blocks to accommodate this plan because there are not enough blocks in the run to completely surround the quilt. This is an advantage, however, because only one "lightest" and only one "darkest" block in the opposite corners of the quilt would not have emphasized the value movement strongly enough.

If you have many different blocks in your run, or if you are using both blocks and mirror images in the quilt, keep track of specific blocks with self-adhesive stickers from the office supply store. Each block can then have a numbered sticker that indicates its placement in the run of blocks. I use a whole (circular) sticker for blocks, a half sticker (semicircle) for mirror image blocks. Do not iron these stickers on the blocks.

13	13	13	12	11	10	9
13	1	1	1	2	2	8
13	2	3	3	3	4	5
12	4	4	5	5	5	6
11	6	6	6	7	7	5
10	7	8	8	8	9	4
9	9	10	10	10	10	3
8	11	11	11	12	12	2
7	12	13	13	13	14	1
6	5	4	3	2	1	1

Quilt progresses from light at the top to dark at the bottom.

USING SEPARATORS TO INTRODUCE COLOR

An alternate way to introduce another color family is to use separators. These are strips cut one inch wide on the straight grain of the fabric. Sew these strips onto the wedges and/or triangles ahead of time. They separate one shape from the next. The colors added with separators can act as accent colors; they add interest to the quilt the way spice adds to the flavor of food.

Blocks with separators can be combined with "no-separator blocks" in your quilt. Maggie Ball's quilt *Psychedelic Pinwheels* (page 82) is a good example of this approach. The separators certainly add visual activity to this surface, making it look as though the blocks are spinning in a whirlpool!

Any given technique or design strategy described up to this point can be used alone or in conjunction with other techniques. Phyllis McFarland did this with her quilt *Where the Sea Dances at Red Rocks* (page 82). Phyllis added separators to blocks that had been produced from a light-to dark run of fabrics. Notice, however, that the light to dark happens only in the wedge shapes. The triangles are a consistent color and value, even though they are from more than one pink fabric.

PSYCHEDELIC PINWHEELS
47" X 47"
Maggie Ball, 1995
Bainbridge Island, Washington

This is a wonderful study of the action
separators can bring to a quilt.

SOARING
57½" X 74"
Veleda Tritremmel Pierre, 1995
Bothell, Washington

A wonderful example of the drama of
separators when they are colored in
contrast to the blocks, and used with
some restraint.

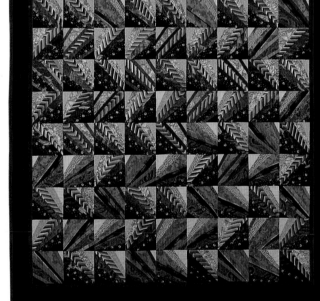

WHERE THE SEA
DANCES AT RED ROCKS
64" X 69"
Phyllis McFarland, 1997
Spokane, Washington

A good study of transition in contrast between the separators and
their background blocks.

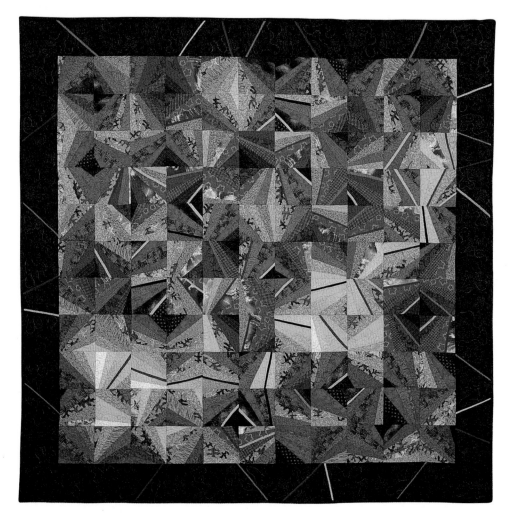

A WALK ON THE WILD SIDE
69" X 69"
Jaqueline Evans, 1996
Albuquerque, New Mexico
Machine quilted by Leta Brazel.

An innovative use of separators; note how letting them "escape" into the border in a much narrower version creates the perfect setting for this fascinating quilt.

In her quilt *Soaring,* Veleda Pierre shows very effective use of separators, since she has used a complementary color for them. Note that Veleda used several fabrics as separators, not just one.

Jacqueline Evans's quilt *A Walk on the Wild Side* is a good example of the excitement that can be added with separators in some but not all blocks. She also allowed narrower separators to "escape" into the border like tossed pickup sticks; this is a very effective way to set off the light and drama of this special quilt.

When used throughout the quilt, separators add a linear element; they often look like a line drawing that has been superimposed on the quilt itself.

Dale MacEwan's quilt *Ripples in the Pond* on page 84 is an example of this linear element, tastefully applied. Using the separators in only a few blocks creates a "quilt arising out of the mist" feeling.

Ria Meszaros certainly has used separators sparingly and for dramatic linear effect in her quilt *Blue Typhoon* (page 84). The separators look like powerful driving raindrops amid the stormy clouds of the rest of her blocks!

You may use one, two, or three separators per block. The number of separators used affects the number of triangles and wedges there are in the block. The blocks look awkward if the shapes are made narrower to accommodate the space taken up by the separators; if the wedges are too narrow, the separators are not distinguishable. Therefore, blocks with separators will have fewer wedges than blocks without separators.

RIPPLES IN THE POND
63" X 63"
Dale MacEwan, 1997
Lantzville, British Columbia, Canada

This quilt shows how separators can be used as a linear element with which to create motifs in the quilt.

Note how effectively Allyn Humphreys has used blocks with separators as border blocks in her quilt *Forest Frenzy* (pictured on page 50). The smaller number of wedges determined by the use of the separators in the border blocks makes this a particularly effective border for this quilt.

Some fabric choices for separators are more successful than others. Separators can be much lighter, much darker, or much brighter than the fabrics of the block's triangles and wedges. Stripes are very effective as separators, especially if they are placed crosswise or at a diagonal to the length of the separator strip.

Using one, two, or three separators presents another set of design options. Using Block A as an example, note how many places there are in the block for a single separator.

BLUE TYPHOON
48" X 40"
Ria Meszaros, 1997
Gold Beach, Oregon

Dramatic use of separators as linear design.

Position possibilities for a single separator in the A block.

If you have two separators per block, you have the following placement choices:

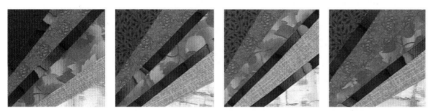

Position possibilities for two separators in the A block; note that the number of total shapes in the block has gone from six to five.

If you use three separators per block, you might move value in the separators as well as in the block. Or, if you use the same fabric for separators in a set of blocks that progress from very light to very dark, the separators will be more obvious in some blocks than in others.

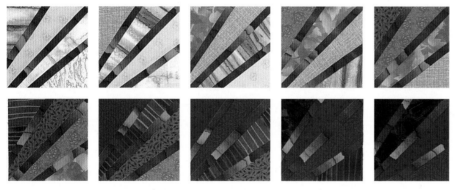

When there are three separators in the block, there are only four shapes. Note that the separators can contrast or blend with the fabrics of the wedges and triangles.

Note that the more separators there are per block, the fewer wedges. Cutting down the number of wedge shapes per block is especially useful when you are using a run of fabrics. This way, you have a greater variety of blocks in your run. For example, if you have ten fabrics in the run, you would be able to make five different kinds of blocks using blocks without separators. If you used three separators, however (which means two triangles and two wedges per block), you would get seven different kinds of blocks in the run.

To determine what fabrics might work as separators, cut one-inch-wide strips from a few selected fabrics, press them in half lengthwise, and lay them onto blocks on your design wall. Then, make a block or two with one separator, a few blocks with two separators, etc. By adding these new blocks a few at a time to the blocks already on your design wall, you will get a feeling for how you want to use blocks with separators.

UNDER THE SEA

42" X 46½"

Callie Smith, 1996

Martinez, California

Stunning use of separators to evoke the "flowing seaweed" feeling; note how the fish swim "among" the separators!

In some quilts, separators are more effective if they are not used in every block. This is certainly the case with Callie Smith's *Under the Sea*. The separators seem to undulate, as seaweed would, in this quilt, and the biggest delight is the way Callie made the school of fish "swim" through these blocks and separators! Notice that the fish are behind some separators and in front of others; some are even swimming over block lines!

Separators may be added to the blocks even after the blocks are sewn together. This approach was used by Maggie Worline in her quilt *Midnight in the Pumpkin Patch*. Note what an effective blending of the two color families Maggie created by slashing the blue blocks at "crazy angles," inserting a narrow strip of orange fabric, then reassembling the block. When using this technique, you must true up the final set of blocks so they are all the same size before you sew them together.

MIDNIGHT IN THE PUMPKIN PATCH

49" X 49"

Maggie Worline, 1995

Camano Island, Washington

Brilliant use of separators to blend blocks of two complementary color families.

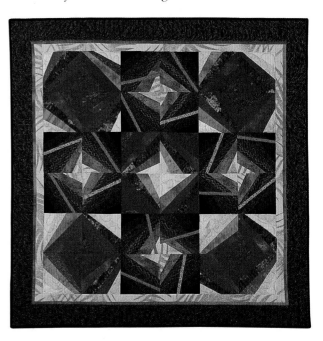

ADDING COLOR WITH ALTERNATE SHAPES

One way to extend the number of blocks that can be made with a given amount of fabric, or to extend the number of different kinds of blocks possible with a given run of fabrics, is to substitute a contrasting fabric for every other shape in the block. This fabric may be much lighter or much darker than the rest of the block fabrics; stripes and large-scale prints are also very effective.

The fabrics you choose for the alternate shape can also vary in value, from block to block or within a given block. This is possible since there are three alternate shapes in Blocks A and B (two wedges and a triangle in each).

There are actually three different blue-and-white striped fabrics used in the alternate shapes in my quilt *Circuit Board*. This occurred because I normally buy only one yard of any one fabric, and I quickly ran out of the first Java Batik I chose as the alternate fabric! One rule of Easy Pieces quilts is that the best thing that can happen to you is that you run out of a given fabric in the process of making your quilt, because then you will be forced to find another fabric in your collection that "sings the same song." This makes you grow as a quiltmaker, and helps you progress in your ability to use fabric effectively in quilts!!

The run of fabrics I started with for this quilt was a run from white/cream through brown to black, with a shot of mauve inserted in the middle-value range. Note that the value strategy was as follows: Starting in the lower right-hand corner, I started progressing dark to light; but about one-third of the way across the quilt, I abruptly switched to the lightest values in the run, and proceeded to get darker from there to the opposite corner.

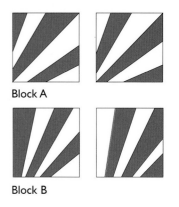

Block A

Block B

CIRCUIT BOARD

57½" X 65"

Margaret J. Miller, 1996

Woodinville, Washington

An example of using a graphic fabric as an alternate shape. Three different blue-and-white stripes were used in this quilt.

**BLACK AND WHITE
AND RED ALL OVER
62" X 62"**

Maurine Roy, 1996
Edmonds, Washington

A good example of combining regular blocks with blocks featuring a particular fabric as alternate shape. Note also the innovative rectangular Easy Pieces blocks Maurine invented to create her border!

Maurine Roy used a combination of "alternate fabric every other wedge" blocks with regular Easy Pieces blocks in her quilt *Black and White and Red All Over.* Note that the high contrast in the blocks that have the alternate fabrics every other wedge adds texture and drama to this quilt.

FOR THE BRAVE OF HEART: SLASHING BLOCKS

An entirely different approach to sprinkling color across a quilt surface is to make two sets of blocks (each from a different color family) and combine them in such a way that both color families appear in each block, but not in predictable ways.

For our example, we will use reds and greens. Take one red block, place a green block on top of it with both right sides up. Slash through the two blocks corner to corner. Then sew the parts back together in such a way that each block has a red portion and a green portion.

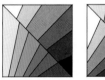
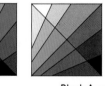
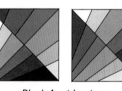

Stacking blocks for slashing and resulting new blocks.

There are a number of ways you could reassemble these four resulting shapes.

A variation on this theme would be to stack and slash other combinations of blocks. Consider stacking and slashing an A block and a B block together—the subtlety in the change in angle could lead to a softening of some patterns. Also, consider stacking and slashing an Easy Pieces block with a single fabric square. How about stacking and slashing a block and its mirror image? Or a Block B with its Reverse? These last two block stacks would be important because of the element of contrast of light to dark within the block and across the quilt. Note that my quilt *Stadium* (page 92) has five different elements: blue blocks, orange blocks, transition (between blue/orange) blocks, blue fabric/pieced fabric blocks, and single fabric squares.

Other slashing possibilities for combinations of blocks.

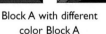

Block A with Block B   Block A with different   Block A with mirror
                                  color Block A   image Block A

There are quite a number of angles at which you could slash the pairs of blocks; every angle will present different design possibilities in the Easy Pieces quilt. Just a few approaches are described below.

1. Slash the block corner to corner. This will make a two-color block, with which you can experiment with all the traditional patterns you know that are based on half-square triangles.

This is the approach Marilyn Badger took to create her quilt *Juicy Fruit* (page 90). Note how skillfully she combined unslashed and slashed Easy Pieces blocks to create the pathways of the "barn raising" type diamonds in this quilt.

JUICY FRUIT
43" X 40"
Marilyn Badger, 1997
Brookings, Oregon

A brilliant study of slashed blocks and multiple color families. Notice the illusion of layers of light in this piece from Marilyn's use of the slashed blocks.

CHAPLIN'S CHECKERS
65" X 71"
Margaret J. Miller, 1997
Woodinville, Washington

This was a study in combining another design element, the checkerboard, with Easy Pieces blocks. The quilt title comes from the fabric used in the border filler triangles, which looks like a row of "Charlie Chaplins."

2. Cut at a 45-degree angle to the edge of the block, but not from corner to corner. Try combining blocks that are slashed at a 45-degree angle, but from different places in the block.

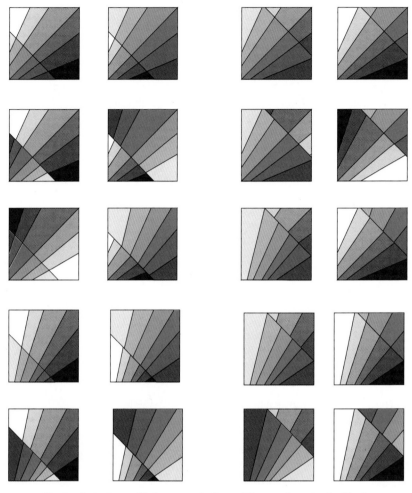

Blocks slashed at a 45-degree angle from different places in the block.

3. Cut at various angles, slashing from one side to an adjacent side.

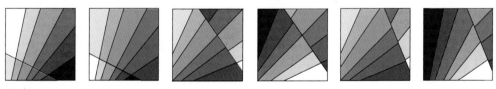

Blocks slashed at various angles.

The blocks for my quilt *Chaplin's Checkers* were slashed from the lower-right corner to one-third of the way down the opposite side (about 2" down from the upper-left corner). Instead of slashing two pieced Easy Pieces blocks at a time, I stacked one Easy Pieces block with a square of a single fabric. This fabric happens to have been shaded from very light grey to black.

STADIUM

48" X 54"

Margaret J. Miller, 1997

Woodinville, Washington

An experiment in slashing, in which a cut was made across the block, from a point 2" down from the top of the left side to one 4" down from the top on the right side.

4. Cut at various angles, slashing from one side of the block to the opposite side. My quilt *Stadium* is an example of a quilt created from blocks that were slashed on a one-third/two-thirds angle.

   To keep the angle consistent from block to block, I drew a block on a sheet of notebook paper. This block had the wedges sketched in so I could place the fabric blocks in the same orientation each time I went to slash them. The slashing angle was drawn in place, with a line that extended well beyond the actual drawing of the block. I later traced the block on the back side of the paper, since I found it necessary to cut angles in both directions for this quilt.

I placed the two blocks to be slashed on top of the paper drawing, aligning the blocks with the edge of the pencil drawing. The slash line was still visible beyond the block, so it was easy to cut the blocks using rotary cutter and acrylic ruler. As the paper guide was used to cut many blocks, the slash line became wider and wider; but this doesn't matter, as long as the general angle is maintained from block to block.

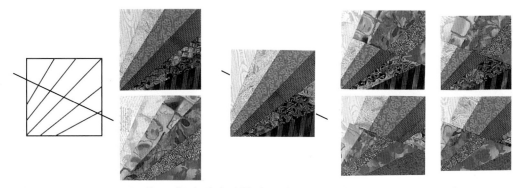

Samples showing one-third/two-thirds slashed blocks, using a paper drawing as a cutting guide.

When the portions are sewn together, a rectangular block is formed. You may use the block in this rectangular form; however, if you want to use this new block in the rotations presented on pages 27-45, true it up to a square shape with your acrylic square.

This approach requires that you begin with larger blocks than you want in the final quilt, because reassembling the blocks after slashing and the squaring-up process reduces the finished size of the original block you cut. For this process I like to start with 7" blocks. See page 96 for cutting guidelines for different size blocks.

5. Making multiple cuts in a pair of blocks introduces another world of quilt design possibilities. In this approach, it is very important to start with cutting wedge blocks much larger than the final desired size. Make a 7" (cut) block to start; this will yield a 6" cut block (5½" finished). To cut the blocks below, a drawing on paper was used as a slashing guide, as described above.

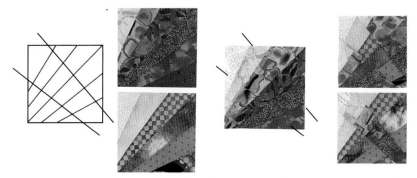

Samples showing double slashing of block, using paper drawing as a cutting guide.

Once the parts are reassembled, true up Block A combinations by aligning the corner-to-corner diagonal on the center seam (it may not align perfectly—that's okay!). If you are using Block B as one or both of your "stack to slash," center a 6" square acrylic ruler in the reassembled rectangular shape, then trim.

Note that the fun of these blocks is playing with value; the arrow up the middle of the block can be in a reverse value gradation to the balance of the block. The contrast in value in the quilt would make the quilt reverberate. To achieve this reversal, stack a block with its mirror image, then double slash as in the diagram on page 93.

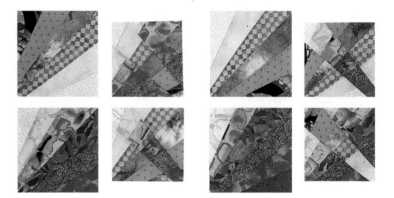

Samples showing two value movement outcomes in double-slashed blocks.

BLENDING COLOR AND VALUE— THE REAL MAGIC OF EASY PIECES QUILTS!

I must remind you that the various color techniques presented in this chapter are meant to be only jumping off places; the real fun of Easy Pieces quilts is making a bunch of blocks from a run of fabrics you think look nice together, then getting them up on the wall to see what happens! Sometimes the subtlety of the blending of colors and values is what is breathtaking about the resultant quilt, which is the case with the following two pieces.

Surely the prize for most subtle blending of color and value of all the quilts in the book goes to Jo Ann Jones for her quilt *Desert At Sunset*. When I received the photo Jo Ann sent me I had to stare at the photo for a long time. Because of her superb blending of color and value, it was hard to tell if in fact she had used Easy Pieces blocks to make this quilt! The blending of the fabrics was accentuated by the quilting design, which further camouflaged the block shape and contents! This quilt is also stunning for the tastefully applied embellishments of nubby yarns, feathers, and beads.

DESERT AT SUNSET
40" X 52"

Jo Ann Jones, 1995

Berkeley, California

This quilt shows how subtle the blending of values can be using Easy Pieces blocks. Yarns, feathers, and beads embellish the design.

RING OF FIRE
40" X 52"
Carol Hanson, 1995
Duluth, Minnesota

Another great example of how blending of color, value, and print scale can be facilitated by the Easy Pieces blocks.

A different kind of blending, but subtle nonetheless, is seen in Carol Hanson's quilt *Ring of Fire*. As you look at this quilt, hunt for all the orange color you can find—you'll be surprised where it all appears! This subtle sprinkling of the warm colors through the predominately cool ones in this quilt make it a thought-provoking piece.

A number of other quilts in this book are good examples of blending of color and value: see La Vonne Horner's *Wisteria Garden* on page 104; Callie Smith's *Under the Sea*, page 86; and Nancy Rasmussen Levy's *Birth of a Nova*, on page 116. Michelle Bowker's *Visions of Isis* is a curious combination of subtle color and value blending; it also expresses a clear pyramid figure against a ground (see page 119). Nola Flynn's *I Don't Do Green, but I Do Do Purple* (on page 115) is a good example of a blended background, on which her orange and purple blocks can float.

flights of
fancy

In this chapter we will explore strategies for creating even more variations with the Easy Pieces blocks; combining Easy Pieces blocks with other patchwork patterns and design elements; using Blocks A and B with their reversals and mirror images in the same quilt, and applying many colors and values to the Easy Pieces quilt. All of these approaches will be simplified by using a number system.

USING DIFFERENT SIZE BLOCKS

Easy Pieces quilt blocks can be cut to any size. The larger the block, the less maneuverability the quiltmaker has to move value across the quilt, because the quilt gets so large so fast. If the block is too small, the triangles and wedges will look like radiating stripes, and the impact of the movement of value in the resulting quilt will be less effective.

The table below gives cutting guidelines for Blocks A and B.

BLOCK SIZE		WEDGES			TRIANGLES
Finished	Cut	First Cut	Cross Cuts	Cut Wedge angle this distance from corner of rectangle	
6½"	7"	10"	3½"-4"	1"	6" x 4"
5½"	6"	9"	3"-3½"	1"	5½" x 4"
4½"	5"	7½"	2½"-3"	¾"	4½" x 3½"
4"	4½"	7"	2½"-3"	¾"	4" x 3"

In general, it is better to start with a block a little larger than you think you need—you can always trim it to size. This is especially true if you are playing with slashing the blocks.

There are two approaches to using multiple-size blocks in a quilt. In the first approach, one block is half the size of its companion block. Such a jump in scale can be jarring, and must be handled carefully. The illustrations on page 97 demonstrate how blocks and half-size blocks might be combined in the same quilt, without having a predictable arrangement of the two.

Combining full-size and half-size blocks.

Combinations with plain fabric squares.

Another more versatile way of combining blocks is to make various size blocks and add fabric so the resulting squares are all the same size. With this approach you can create another visual level in the quilt—the blocks can appear to be "floating" in space or on another background. Or, you could have regular blocks "breaking into" arrangements of these smaller blocks to give the impression that the smaller blocks are breaking away from the main body of blocks.

COMBINING MULTIPLE TYPES OF BLOCKS

There are literally thousands of ways to combine all or some of the design elements presented so far in one quilt. At the beginning of this book, we presented twelve possibilities for patterns that each of these two blocks could form if they were rotated in place on the wall. But in addition, we have the mirror images of Blocks A and B, and reverse B blocks with which to create variations on the original design themes. Then, adding more color families complicates the picture even further!

Before reading any farther, remember you need not follow any of these pathways to your ultimate quilt design. Any strategies presented in this book are meant only as suggestions to help you get your blocks onto the wall quickly. Then the real fun begins as you fine tune your arrangement on the wall.

Using this approach, Pat Johnston arrived at her quilt *Wedgetivity* (page 54) by making a set of A blocks and a set of B blocks from the same pool of fabrics, and playing with them with magnificent results on her design wall.

If, however, you like an organized strategy to start with, this chapter is for you. Or, if you are the kind of quilter who freezes when presented with so many decisions to make, this chapter will help you break down the forest of possibilities into categories of options.

General Approach

When experimenting with new ways of sprinkling shapes or colors across a quilt surface, I find it helpful to start with a neutral system so I can focus on the overall plan for the quilt, without agonizing about specific color or design content of the blocks I'm working with. Two neutral systems I have found helpful are shaded squares on graph paper, and numbers used to indicate different kinds of blocks in a series.

1. Using Shaded Diagrams

You started experimenting at the beginning of this book with only one kind of block; you made an experimental set of A blocks or B blocks. We are going to begin with that basic set.

Place your basic blocks on the wall in whatever rotation is pleasing to you. Referring to the shaded diagrams on pages 57-58, consider the light squares as your basic set of blocks on the wall. For the shaded blocks, substitute one of the following:

1) another color family
2) mirror image blocks of Block A or Block B
3) reverse B blocks
4) Block B (if you made A blocks to start; or vice-versa)
5) block rotated ¼ turn
6) block turned upside down
7) block rotated ¾ turn

2. The Number System

On pages 79-81 a number of strategies were presented for applying a run of blocks to a given quilt surface. The numbers referred to blocks made according to a swatch sheet, in which number one referred to the block that began with fabric number one from the swatch sheet; number two was the block that began with fabric number two, etc.

The number system can also refer to a set of transition blocks, where number one could refer to a block with one shape from the other color family; number two would be the block with two shapes from the other color family, etc. Note that with Block A, block number three would look like half-square triangles, as the corner-to-corner seam would divide the two color families evenly in the block.

The numbered diagrams presented are quite simple strategies; you may find that in real blocks better blending occurs when you use two different kinds of blocks for any one element of your design strategy. For example, in the diagrams at left note that in the upper diagram, a straightforward "barn raising" arrangement has been interpreted in numbers. With Easy Pieces blocks, you may find that the lower arrangement is more effective. This was the case in the quilt *Kerry's Hearts II* (page 101).

Remember that this number system refers only to the type of block in each position: what pattern in the total quilt that block makes by rotating it in place is an entirely different design process.

8	8	7	6	5	6	7	8	8
8	7	6	5	4	5	6	7	8
7	6	5	4	3	4	5	6	7
6	5	4	3	2	3	4	5	6
5	4	3	2	1	2	3	4	5
6	5	4	3	2	3	4	5	6
7	6	5	4	3	4	5	6	7
8	7	6	5	4	5	6	7	8
8	8	7	6	5	6	7	8	8

9	8	9	8	6	8	9	8	9
8	9	8	7	4	7	8	9	8
9	8	6	5	2	5	6	8	9
8	7	4	3	1	3	4	7	8
6	5	2	1	1	1	2	5	6
8	7	4	3	1	3	4	7	8
9	8	6	5	2	5	6	8	9
8	9	8	7	4	7	8	9	8
9	8	9	8	6	8	9	8	9

Use numbered diagrams for block placement.

COMBINING OTHER DESIGN ELEMENTS AND EASY PIECES BLOCKS

You might think from reading the book thus far that all Easy Pieces quilts have pieced Easy Pieces blocks throughout. This is not so. Another whole world of design possibilities opens up when you consider adding other design elements (perhaps from traditional patchwork books) to a group of Easy Pieces blocks.

1. **Panel Prints.** There are many panel prints on the market that could suggest a theme for your quilt. Mary Ann Musgrove was commissioned to make a baby quilt for the new grandson of two marine biologist friends. Mary Ann began her quilt with a batik panel print of jumping Orca whales. The fabrics she chose were meant to suggest the foamy ocean, and her arrangement was not meant as a recognizable pattern, but rather as a representation of the waters churned up by the frolicking whales, which she accomplished masterfully!

BABY QUILT FOR
BENJAMIN
44" X 54"
Mary Ann Musgrove, 1996
La Conner, Washington
Collection of Benjamin Owen
Gilvar-Parke, Austin, Texas.

A good example of not using any pattern at all, but trying to express a certain effect, such as the frothiness of the ocean, with Easy Pieces blocks.

Good use of an accent fabric in the middle of the block to form a medallion focus for this quilt. Though this quilt has a very African feel to it, there is not one truly African fabric used in its making!

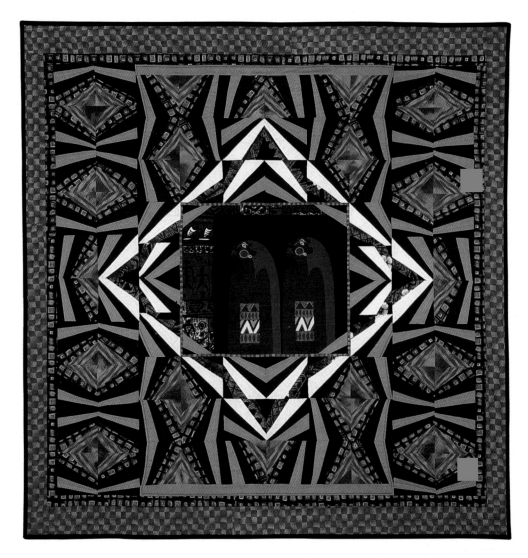

Maurine Roy, in her quilt *Sisters*, did not use a light-to-dark arrangement in the A and B blocks she used to frame this panel print. Also note the dramatic effect she achieved by using a small number of different fabrics, especially the white fabric that formed the medallion around the panel print.

2. **Traditional Blocks.** *Kerry's Hearts II* began as a huge set of blocks sent by friends wishing Kerry Hoffman Smith a speedy recovery after heart surgery (thus the heart theme of the blocks). A border was sewn onto each of the 6" blocks so that they could be considered 8" finished blocks; this approach enabled me to combine 4" Easy Pieces blocks to set them off. The friendship blocks were first offset from each other so together they formed a giant heart shape in the middle of the quilt. Then the small Easy Pieces blocks were made from a run of light-to-dark teal fabrics; the number system was used to determine their placement.

The layered look in the corners was not something I anticipated ahead of time, but what a delight it was to discover the first time I looked at this quilt through the reducing glass!

KERRY'S HEARTS II
79" X 80"
Margaret J. Miller and
Kerry's Friends, 1997
Woodinville, Washington

Blocks gathered by Marion Shelton. Collection of Kerry I. Hoffman Smith, Bainbridge Island, Washington. Machine quilted by Roxanne Carter. Eight-inch sampler blocks were framed by 4" Easy Pieces blocks; a series of nineteen fabrics was used in sequence to create this setting.

3. **Single Fabric Shapes.** Some rotations of Easy Pieces blocks can be given some breathing space by substituting single fabric squares. This is obviously more effective with smaller blocks than with larger (7" or more) ones.

In her quilt *Fire and Ice* (page 45), Doris Northcutt made a weaving of a linear pattern much more effective by spreading it out a bit with single fabric squares. This pattern is also intriguing because you sometimes see the weaving pattern first, but if you turn away from the quilt and look back at it, sometimes the whirling pinwheel stars emerge (look at the gray squares, with the very light triangles north, south, east, and west of it). Other times, the smallest stars, where the four lightest triangles come together, are more obvious.

The tone of this chapter is such that you might think that only organized approaches work when you have a pile of Easy Pieces blocks in your hand and a blank design wall in front of you, but do remember that any design strategies presented in this book are only jumping-off places! Once you start playing with a "real life" set of blocks, you won't need to be reminded of this! The challenge is to keep a photographic record of the hundreds of quilts you will create on your design wall, so you can return to these ideas later and flesh them out into yet another Easy Pieces quilt!

CHAPTER FIVE

sashing strips
and borders

You can see there are thousands of ways of arranging the Easy Pieces quilt blocks on your design wall. In this chapter we want to take the designing process a couple steps further, and consider sashing strips and borders to enhance the "action" in the middle of your quilt.

SASHING STRIPS

The patterns Easy Pieces blocks make depend on their being placed edge to edge. Separating each block from its mate with a sashing strip, as is done in traditional quilts, would interrupt the flow of design with Easy Pieces blocks. However, by reaching for the unexpected in the manner in which you apply sashing strips and by their content, you will see that coming up with a pattern for the blocks is just the beginning of the Easy Pieces story.

Sashing strips, as used to separate only selective groups of blocks, can add organization to a design that is otherwise less than successful. This was the case with my quilt *Go for the Green*. This quilt was an experiment in restricting myself to one line of fabrics (P&B Textiles' "Basics" collection). I wanted to work with multiple values and a run of colors, which in this case was peach to orange to red to purple to green. Furthermore, I wanted to create a medallion quilt that was not a typical medallion; i.e., not centered in the quilt, and not symmetrical on all four sides. These goals I did accomplish, so I sewed the blocks together and was unhappy with the result. However, taking the quilt apart, inserting sashing strips, and adding the border, much improved the quilt. The sashing strips in this quilt act as a "windowpane" through which you are looking at the actual blocks beyond. The elements that were distracting in the original quilt are intriguing in this version, with sashing strips added. The bright yellow setting squares were used to "lift" the windowpane farther from the background blocks.

GO FOR THE GREEN

75" X 98"

Margaret J. Miller, 1997

Woodinville, Washington

Machine quilted by Patsi Hanseth,

Mt. Vernon, Washington.

A series of twenty-four fabrics was used in
sequence to create the blocks for this quilt.

WISTERIA GARDEN
58" X 67"

La Vonne J. Horner, 1995
Superior, Wisconsin

Another great example of blending value
and texture using Easy Pieces blocks.

SOME LIKE IT COLD
45" X 45"

Marion G. Mackey, 1997
West Chester, Pennsylvania

The luminosity in this quilt is
accentuated by the colors chosen
for the setting squares.

Multiple Widths

Consider using more than a single width of sashing strip; some narrow, some wider. In her quilt *Wisteria Garden*, La Vonne Horner has taken this approach as she inserted sashing strips between groups of four blocks. Note that the variation in width of the sashing strips, especially the very narrow ones, adds drama to the already breathtaking movement of value La Vonne has achieved with her blocks.

In her quilt *Some Like it Cold*, Marion Mackey has also used various width sashing strips, but note the excitement she added with the setting squares. Note also that her sashing strips sometimes separate pairs of blocks and sometimes come between single blocks.

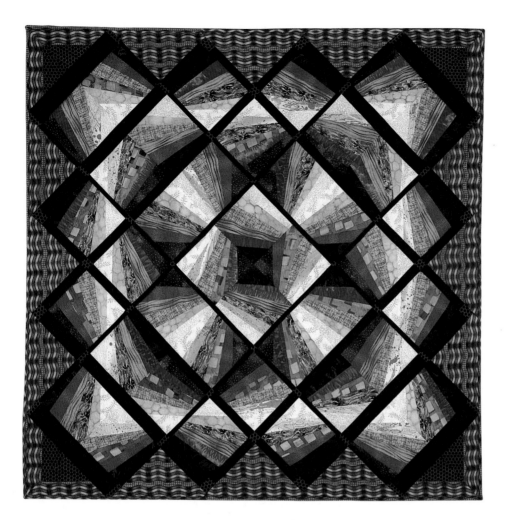

SEATTLE SUMMER—
STILL RAINING
50" X 50"
Margaret J. Miller, 1997
Woodinville, Washington

In this quilt I wanted to feature
Reverse B blocks and variation in
sashing strip width.

My quilt *Seattle Summer—Still Raining* (project instructions pages 127-131) also features graduated width sashing strips. The innermost ones are one-half inch finished, and graduate in size by half an inch to the outermost ones, which measure two inches finished. Note how this graduated size intensifies the focus on the design in the center of the quilt.

Maneuvering Color and Value

Another way to reach for the unexpected is to move value from light to dark in the sashing strips, perhaps in a different manner than the light is manipulated in the quilt itself. For example, if the quilt is very light in the center, and gets darker as you approach the borders (like Avis Caddell's *Diamonds and Sapphires*, page 70), imagine how different the quilt would look if the sashing strips did just the opposite—went from very dark in the center to light at the edges of the quilt. If, in addition, the sashing strips were narrower in the center and wider toward the quilt's edges the effect of the sashing strips would be even more dramatic.

In her quilt *Desert Reflections* (page 106), Veleda Pierre, used only narrow sashing strips in her quilt, but notice how effectively she manipulated color in them. The pattern of color seems to suggest a maze, and the one gold fabric with the wavy line makes the quilt take on a desert mirage look. These sashing strips are especially effective in this piece because of the way Veleda has used the same two colors in the border.

DESERT REFLECTIONS
51½" X 52"
Veleda Tritremmel Pierre, 1997
Bothell, Washington

A novel use of color in sashing strips, complemented well by the same colors in the narrow border.

Dana Bard has also used multiple colors in her sashing strips in a dramatic manner. A first glance at her quilt *Kansas* seems to reveal multiple layers, each layer separated by a different color sashing strip. However, when you see the quilt closer, and note the heavy beading around each of the little gold setting squares, you realize that the green sashing strips are actually separating individual pieced Easy Pieces Sunflowers.

KANSAS
64½" X 63½"
Dana M. Bard, 1996
Chico, California

A most innovative border treatment, and multiple "layers" created by sashing strips.

Other Design Elements as Sashing Strips

You don't have to use only single strips of fabric to separate groups of blocks; consider using checkerboards. The illustrations below show some of the ways sashing strips could be "checkered"—from block to block, or in multiples beneath each block.

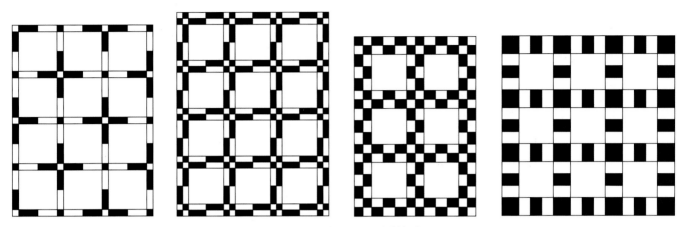

The empty spaces in these diagrams could be for a single block, or for a group of blocks.

BORDERS

It is extremely important to reserve some creative energy for the design of the borders of quilts; good quilts can be ruined by a poorly thought-out border, and very ordinary quilts can be made spectacular by the design of a good one. In this section we will consider some springboards for good border design.

Let's start with the definition of a border. Unfortunately, many people think that a border is something rigid to "hold the quilt blocks in," like the wooden frame on a painting. This is what leads so many quiltmakers to finish a quilt, then put one or more single strips of fabric all the way around the quilt (especially if they have used a single print to choose all the fabrics for this quilt). *I'm not saying one should never again put single (or multiple) strips of fabric around a pieced quilt*, neither am I saying that this type of simple border is never appropriate, but rather, I am urging you to consider some border alternatives!

The definition we present here is that a border is "an area in which the quilt can come to a gradual visual close." In that spirit then, we will consider the following ways to reach for the unexpected:

1. quilts on a field of plain fabric
2. quilt design forming the border
3. orientation of quilt other than parallel to edges
4. camouflaging where quilt stops and border begins
5. letting the action—and color—"escape" into border
6. manipulating value to form border area
7. multiple borders; the border within a border idea
8. other shapes as border blocks
9. other design elements as springboards for border design.

Quilts on a Field of Plain Fabric

The first option to consider is to lay the pieced quilt onto a field of a single (unpieced) fabric. This is the approach Claudia Myers took with her huge quilt *Shazam!*. Note how effectively she used both color families that appeared in the quilt—the red border is on the opposite edge from the red motif in the quilt, and the blue border is opposite the blue motif.

San Diego quiltmaker m.j. Judy Hopkins also placed her quilt *Source* on a field of background fabric, but in a most innovative position. This askew positioning of the quilt in relation to its perimeter certainly takes advantage of the diagonal motifs in Judy's quilt.

SHAZAM!

96" X 96"

Claudia Clark Myers, 1995

Duluth, Minnesota

Though this piece (by far the largest in this book!) is machine pieced and machine quilted, the gold star and streak shapes are hand appliquéd.

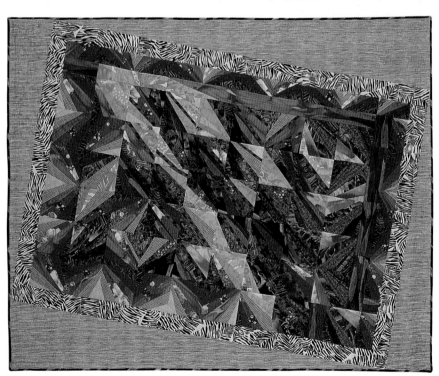

SOURCE

52" X 65"

m.j. Judy Hopkins, 1995

San Diego, California,

A most refreshing positioning of the quilt askew within its perimeters. Note the use of narrow fabric strips and partial blocks that form inner borders on two sides.

Patchwork Design as a Border

Another possibility is to add no formal border at all, but rather let the design itself "finish the action" of the main quilt. My quilt *Labyrinth* falls into this category. The zigzag pattern is the actual close of the quilt; the alternately dark and medium triangles are a field on which that zigzag border rests. The triangles are merely devices to provide a straight edge for the quilt.

Shirley Jan's quilt *Crystal* is another example of a zigzag motif (Pattern Eight, with blocks and mirror image blocks, page 35) used as a border, but this time for a rectangular quilt. Note how she has allowed her zigzag to "fade out" on the upper-left and lower-right corners. This quilt is also an example of making the final shape of the quilt something other than a square or rectangle; in this case, an oblong octagon.

LABYRINTH
62" X 62"
Margaret J. Miller, 1996
Woodinville, Washington

This quilt was an experiment in using the lightest wedge of the B block as a drawing tool to create motifs on the quilt surface.

CRYSTAL
52" X 78"
Shirley Jan, 1996
Riverside, Illinois

Shirley created her more angular zigzag border using B blocks and their mirror image.

IFUGAO

52" X 52"

Celeste F. Delostrinos, 1997

Seattle, Washington

Tribesmen in the mountain province of the Philippines carry wooden shields carved with symbols of power similar to this design.

My quilt *Persimmon* (pictured on page 33) is another example of a zigzag pattern used as border. In this quilt, however, the zigzag is made with two rows of blocks. This quilt actually began with the placement of those two border rows on the design wall, as I had seen this zigzag pattern in one of the photographs of patterns I had experimented with early on. Once the border was up, I had to go back to square one and decide what to put in the middle of the quilt! The zigzag was created with a run of fabrics that went from deep teal, which lightened and transitioned in the light area, to a fabric that had both pale turquoise and pale peach in it. Then the run of peach fabrics got darker, ending in a deep burgundy. Note that the solution to blending these two very strong colors in the corner was to use separators.

Celeste Delostrinos has created a similar situation in her quilt *Ifugao*. Note that the design of the quilt ends with the last colored wedge (the pink ones, not the white ones, which are actually the color of the first wedge of the border blocks). By adding a single fabric border of the very light fabric, she has made her quilt an "island."

Another approach to patchwork design as a border has to do with looking at patterns made with photocopies of Easy Pieces designs, or photographs of your own Easy Pieces creations on your design wall, and considering cutting out the middle of the design to form the border. This cutting out could be along horizontal and vertical block lines, along a series of corner-to-corner A block lines, or along a zigzag line that leaves a medallion hole in the middle. A number of Easy Pieces patterns lend themselves to this approach. Just a few of them appear below.

Cutting out the middle of the design to form the border.

Cutting out the middle along block lines.

MEMORIES OF POPPIES
PAST
56" X 66"
Beckie Franck Hansen, 1997
Mukilteo, Washington

A stunning illusion that there is a black quilt set askew onto a red one behind it, all achieved by the sprinkling of color in the blocks.

Orientation of the Quilt Other than Parallel to the Edges

We have already seen this approach in m.j. Judy Hopkins's quilt *Source* (see page 108). A similar visual effect was achieved by Beckie Hansen in her quilt *Memories of Poppies Past*, but she used a very different approach. Beckie created the illusion that there is a rectangular black quilt set askew onto a red background, yet all the reds and blacks are in the form of Easy Pieces blocks. The positioning of the large appliquéd and trapuntoed poppies are a smashing finishing touch to this quilt.

IRIS THROUGH THE
WINDOW
38" X 44"
Patsi Hanseth, 1997
Mt. Vernon, Washington

A novel way to frame an appliqué
piece using Easy Pieces blocks.

In this same category of border options we could consider changing the location of the quilt within the perimeter of the quilt. In other words, instead of placing the quilt equidistant from each edge, look what Patsi Hanseth did in her quilt *Iris Through the Window*. She not only placed the obvious focus of the quilt, the appliquéd iris block, closer to the upper-left corner of the quilt, but she also used partial Easy Pieces blocks to make her focus block octagonal rather than square.

Dana Bard presents another variation on this theme in her quilt *Kansas* (page 106). Dana's border is refreshing because the element that gives her quilt a theme, the appliquéd sunflower, is actually one of the borders, and is not even located anywhere near the center of this quilt! This quilt is a good example of reaching for the unexpected in border design: creating the same plan for three edges of the quilt, something entirely different on the fourth edge!

Camouflaging Where the Quilt Stops and the Border Begins

This is perhaps the most effective way of reaching for the unexpected in border design. By diffusing the delineation between quilt and border, you make the viewer take in the whole piece, rather than focusing on any one single design element of your quilt.

In her quilt *Fuschia Sizzle*, Lucy Zeldenrust has used this approach masterfully. Note that she arranged the dark and light portions of a theme fabric carefully, to highlight the quilt center with contrast. The camouflage between quilt and border was accomplished using a partial Easy Pieces block.

FUSCHIA SIZZLE

51" X 51"

Lucy Zeldenrust, 1996

Two Rivers, Wisconsin

Though there are relatively few (44) Easy Pieces blocks in this quilt, they are given more importance by the width and the movement of light to dark in the border fabric Lucy applied.

My quilt *Go for the Green* (page 103) shows another way to camouflage where the quilt stops and the border begins. The deep green fabric used as sashing strips seems to end in the square shapes in the border, thus leading the eye off the edge of the quilt.

Letting the Action Escape into the Border

Another very effective border technique is to let the action—or the color—escape into the border in unpredictable ways. This was accomplished in my quilt *Circuit Board* (page 87) with the "slashes" of color that weave in and out of the three-fabric border. Note that there are no fabrics that appear both in the border and in the center of the quilt; this also breaks the commonly held rule that one must have enough of one of the quilt's fabrics to use as a border!

In her quilt *I Don't Do Green, But I Do Do Purple*, Nola Flynn has added strips of fabric for her border that would normally be too narrow to be an effective border. But since they are echoes of fabrics already in the blocks, they now complete the area in which the quilt comes to a visual close. This process begins at least two rows in from any edge. Note at the top of the quilt that since the border fabric is used in the blocks, the blocks become almost filigreed as they approach the actual border strips.

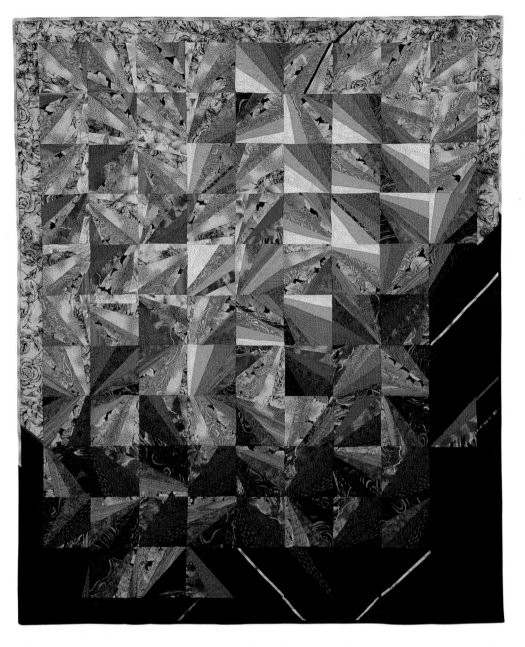

I DON'T DO GREEN,
BUT I DO DO PURPLE
54" X 65"

Nola Flynn, 1996

Eureka, California

This quilt features blocks that seem
to disappear into the background
fabric of the upper-left corner by
using that same fabric in the blocks
near that area.

Veleda Pierre used a similar approach in her quilt *Desert Reflections* (page 106). However, the two fabrics she used in her border strips appear in only in the sashing strips of the quilt, not the blocks themselves. Veleda's border, then, completes the stable gridwork, through which you see the undulating blocks behind.

Manipulating Color and Value to Create the Border Area

The subtitle for this section could be "Creating a Quilt that Doesn't Need a Border." Sometimes the manipulation of color or value alone makes it clear that the quilt has come to its natural close.

This is certainly the case with Nancy Rasmussen Levy's *Birth of A Nova* (page 116). Though she manipulates many colors in a small quilt, Nancy has employed a value strategy of light in the center, gradually darkening as the eye approaches the edge of the quilt. The degree and amount of dark values on the outer edge of this quilt declare that it is complete.

BIRTH OF A NOVA
36" X 48"

Nancy Rasmussen Levy, 1995
Pleasant Hill, California

A spectacular example of blending
color families and a wide range of
value with the Easy Pieces A blocks.

The process of assigning values to the outermost row of blocks in my quilt *Sunrise, Sunset* (page 76) has already been discussed (page 75). Sometimes merely a reversal of value can declare the visual finish of the quilt.

Multiple Borders: The Border-Within-a-Border Idea

Diane Ross made a quilt with multiple borders, entitled *Peaz 'n' Lilies,* even though each successive border is not determined by a separate row of blocks or strips of fabric. Note that the dark pinks form one border (embellished with the couched, narrow gold cord, which rides the surface in unpredictable ways). The next border would be the lighter pinks; the narrow accent band of teal before the final print strips all work together to set off the sixteen blocks in the center of this quilt.

PEAZ 'N' LILIES
35" X 35"
Diane N. Ross, 1997
Woodinville, Washington

An effective use of B blocks and their
mirror images to create a border
within a border.

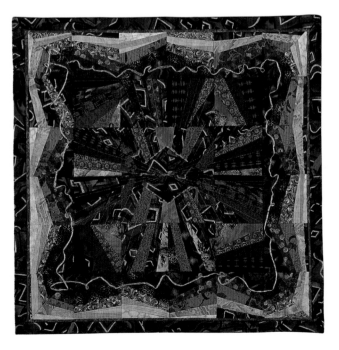

CROSS ROADS

38" X 38"

Gail Sheirbon, 1997

Santa Clara, California

Machine quilted by Kathy Sandbach.

An effective blending of two color families throughout the quilt; also, interesting use of checkerboarding to camouflage where the quilt stops and the border begins.

Gail Shierbon also used multiple borders in her *Cross Roads* quilt. The checkerboard inner border certainly qualifies as an element that is beginning to "stop the action" in the quilt. The zigzag border formed by the narrow orange strips is a very important element to tie this quilt together. Without those narrow strips, this would have looked like an orange quilt with a blue border. Adding the touch of orange in the outer border finishes the color sentence begun in the middle of this quilt.

Other Design Elements in Border Design

As you peruse the pages of this book, you will see a number of additional design elements that made for some interesting border treatments.

In her quilt *Forest Frenzy* (page 50), Allyn Humphreys restricted her use of separators to the border area only, thus creating a crispness to the border that is in contrast to the muted softness of the dancing pinwheels in the center of this quilt.

Maurine Roy's *Lights on My Christmas Tree* (page 66), has a narrow red border that isn't a typical strip-pieced one. Maurine took some leftover B blocks from her quilt, cut them in half, and sewed them end to end; the result is a delightful surprise as you examine the various elements of this quilt!

A similar surprise comes at the edge of my quilt *Rainbow Blues*, on page 23. This quilt was actually started to use up the leftovers from *Go for the Green* (page 103). Since the wedges and triangles assembled for a 6" B block can accommodate cutting a 6½" block, I cut 6" x 6½" rectangles as the border units. The difference is subtle, but important. The corner blocks were cut 6½" square.

Maurine Roy took rectangular blocks to the limit with her quilt *Black and White and Red All Over* (see page 88). She created her own version of a large rectangular Easy Pieces block to create the mid-sections of her border. The change in the angle produced by such blocks is a wonderful fluid contrast to the staccato center design.

With the above ideas now dropped into the pond of your border-conscious mind, may you reach for the unexpected in designing border areas not only for your Easy Pieces quilts, but other future quilts as well!

quilting
the easy pieces quilt

just when you think you've made more decisions and chosen among more options than should be humanly possible in deciding on an arrangement for your Easy Pieces quilt blocks, you are faced with another forest of possibilities when it comes to deciding how to quilt your quilt! In Easy Pieces quilts, the quilting design is not determined by nor limited to patterns suggested by the seamlines within the block, nor the seams that hold the blocks together.

Easy Pieces quilts can be quilted by hand or by machine. If your quilting pattern involves crossing a lot of seams (of which there are many in most Easy Pieces quilts), machine quilting is probably a wiser choice.

For quilts in general, and for Easy Pieces quilts in particular, I like to create quilting designs that disguise where one block stops and its neighbor begins, and where some of the shapes within the block are joined. However, to begin my machine quilting, I generally stitch a grid "in the ditch" of the block seams to hold the layers of the quilt sandwich in place before beginning the "fun" machine quilting!

The quilts in this book ran the gamut of quilting design—from very little to lots of quilting, done both by hand and by machine. The quilt which took the cake for the quilting most unrelated to the patchwork design, and for the quilt with the most quilting in it, was Michelle Bowker's *Vision of Isis*. The strong suggestion of a pyramid shape on the front inspired the overall Egyptian quilting motifs, which were drawn on paper and machine quilted from the back of the quilt by Angela Haworth.

My friend Patsi Hanseth quilted my quilt *Persimmon* (see page 33) on her large-track quilting machine. She quilted large soft flower shapes in each of the offset checkers in the middle of the quilt, which certainly softened the whole design, and helped the design flow into the border.

Marilyn Badger also has a professional quilting machine, and her husband has invented and markets an attachment for it that enables her to machine quilt perfect circles. Her pattern of concentric circles over her quilt *Juicy Fruit* (pictured on page 90) certainly changed the character of this otherwise very angular medallion.

Quilting design can really accentuate the blending of colors and values. When I first received a photograph of Jo Ann Jones's *Desert at Sunset* (pictured on page 95), I spent a long time looking at the photograph, trying to decide if this quilt was made of Easy Pieces blocks at all. The flowing nature of the quilting lines really disguised where one block stopped and the next one began.

VISION OF ISIS

67½" X 53½"

Michelle Bowker, 1996

Duluth, Minnesota

Machine quilted by Angela Haworth. Another superb example of blending, but this time with a clearly delineated pyramid shape.

Back view of VISION OF ISIS, showing Angela Haworth's superb machine quilting, which depicts many Egyptian motifs.

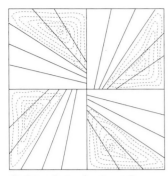

Quilting design for *Forest Frenzy.*

Planning the quilting design for Easy Pieces quilts has to do with the flow of light and the flow of color pattern, much more than the position of the block seams. In order to accentuate the dancing pinwheels in Allyn Humphreys's quilt *Forest Frenzy* (page 50), I quilted irregular spirals in a dark but variegated thread over the last three shapes of each block, and only stitched in the ditch between the first three wedges, allowing them to puff out.

Some quilt designs have obvious distinct sections, so you can have unrelated quilting designs in different areas of the quilt. My quilt *Stadium* (page 92) had obvious orange and blue zigzags across the main section. The quilting design in the orange zigzag ended up looking like rows of people, hence the title for the quilt. In the blue section, the predictable plan would have been to quilt lines parallel to the edges of the blue zigzag, but I purposely changed the angle of those lines, and used stipple quilting to highlight the shape they delineated.

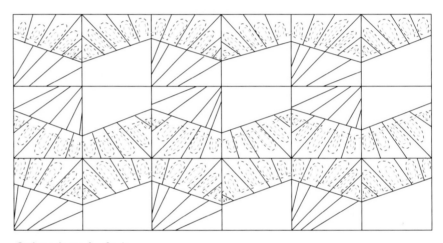

Quilting design for *Stadium.*

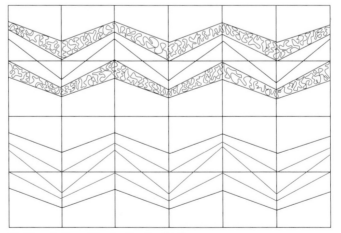

Quilting design with stippling for *Stadium.*

To open your eyes to more quilting possibilities, take your photocopies of the designs in Appendix B and put a piece of tracing paper over each one. With a fine-tip colored marker, draw quilting lines that purposely cross or ignore the seamlines in the pattern. Start by focusing on only single blocks, then groups of blocks, and finally entire patterns. Just a few suggestions appear on the next page.

Quilting design possibilities that ignore the seamlines.

When your quilt blocks are in place on the wall, take a photograph in which the quilt really fills the viewfinder of the camera. Get at least a 4" print made (a 5" x 7" enlargement would be even better). By placing tracing paper or transparent plastic (such as page protector envelopes) over the photograph, you can try multiple possibilities for quilting design using a pencil (on the paper) or a fine, felt-tipped marker (on the paper or plastic).

Don't run out of creative energy before you plan your quilting design. A given quilt can be enhanced or diminished by the pattern of quilting lines that change the look of the pieced surface. Have as much fun deciding your quilting pattern as you did arranging and rearranging the blocks on the wall in the first place!

CHAPTER SEVEN projects
for you

for those of you who would like more guidance in the making of your first Easy Pieces quilt, this chapter presents directions for two different quilt projects. Together, they offer a variety of quilt possibilities, and feature all the different types of blocks presented in this book. One project features a directional pattern with the A block only; the second quilt incorporates Block B with Reverse Block B and sashing strips. Both projects feature blocks on point. Specific fabric yardage requirements are listed with each project. *NOTE: Yardages given are MINIMUM and based on 42″ width. You may choose to buy a little more for safety's sake! You can always sew the leftovers together to make the quilt backing!*

General Supplies
- Sewing machine
- Thread appropriate to fabrics chosen
- Iron and ironing board
- Rotary cutting equipment: mat, cutter, acrylic ruler (6″ x 24″), and acrylic square appropriate for block size of project
- Fabrics for quilt top, backing, and binding
- Quilt batting
- Reducing glass
- Camera

Review the general cutting and sewing instructions for Blocks A and B on pages 11-22; any specialty cutting is explained in the directions with each quilt project.

AFTERNOON AT THE
ZOO
39" X 39"
Margaret J. Miller, 1997
Woodinville, Washington

This quilt is very similar to my quilt *Polliwogs* shown on page 9. The idea was to start with only the basic set of sixteen A blocks and sixteen mirror images, and see what kind of quilt would result from the basic cutting directions. Edge-filler triangles were used to make a border.

AFTERNOON AT THE ZOO

Additional tools required: 6" and 12" acrylic squares

Cut Block Size: 6"   Finished Block Size: 5½"

Number of Blocks Required: 40 blocks

(24 A blocks plus 16 mirror image blocks) plus 20 border/corner triangles

Yardage

Six fabrics ranging in value from light (Fabric 1) to dark (Fabric 6).

A seventh fabric for border triangles.

Values 1 and 6: ⅓ yard each

Values 2, 3, 4, 5: ⅝ yard each

Border/Corner Triangles: ⅝ yard

Backing: 1½ yards

Binding: Your choice, depending on whether you make straight or double bias binding

Cutting Triangles and Wedges

Triangles: Values 1 and 6

See pages 11-12, To Cut Triangles.

Be sure to stack leftovers in one area of your work table. You will be cutting more shapes from them after a basic set of thirty-two blocks has been made.

Wedges: Values 2, 3, 4, 5

See page 13, To Cut Wedges

NOTE: In the example, Fabric 3 was a stripe. In order to get the stripes to end up crossways on my wedges, I first folded the fabric so there were four layers, and cut a 14" strip. I subcut that into two 9" strips, stacked them together, and from that stack cut one 3½" x 9" rectangle and one 3" x 9" rectangle. Photographs of this process appear on pages 14-15.

Sewing Blocks

Follow general instructions on pages 16-20.

Cutting Leftover Fabrics for Eight More Blocks

Cut the following from your "leftover" strips (the ones you pinned after cutting the final subcut, per general instructions, page 12).

Values 1 and 6: (four layers) Cut one 4" subcut.

TURN ALL RECTANGLES RIGHT SIDE UP, align them, then cut the following diagonals (note that there are different directions for lights than for darks):

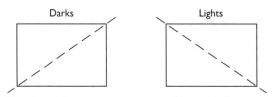

Darks   Lights

Cut diagonally corner to corner to form triangles.

Value 2: (four layers) Make one more 3½" subcut.

TURN ALL 3½" x 9" FABRIC RECTANGLES RIGHT SIDE UP, align, and cut the following diagonal to form wedges:

Cut diagonally to form wedges.

Value 3: Cut same as for Value 2.

Value 4: (four layers) Make one 3" subcut. Turn all 3" x 9" rectangles right sides up and cut same wedge diagonal as in Value 5.

Value 5: Cut same as for Value 2.

Arrange triangles and wedges lighter toward darker on sewing table. Assemble blocks using chain piecing methods, though no wedges or triangles will turn up wrong sides up, so there will be nothing to flip out of the way.

Cutting Border and Corner Triangles

Fold fabric so you are cutting through four layers. Using the larger acrylic square, cut out a 9½" square. Open out leftover fabric, cut one more 9½" square, and add to the stack of four already cut.

Cut squares corner to corner on both diagonals. This gives you twenty triangles.

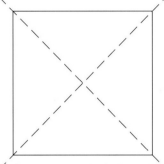

Cut squares on both diagonals.

Quilt Construction

Place blocks and mirror image blocks on the design wall.

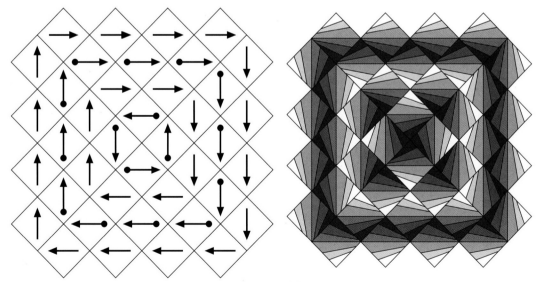

Block Placement

Block Rotation

Block placement options for four central blocks. Notice how different the quilt looks when you merely rotate the central four blocks a number of ways.

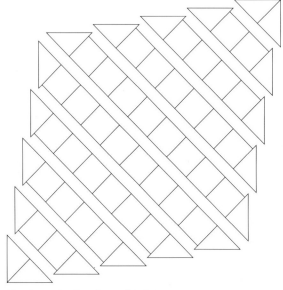

Sewing order for diagonal rows.

Sew together diagonal rows; press seams between blocks open; replace rows on design wall. The border and corner triangles purposely extend beyond the finished corners of the blocks—they will be trimmed later.

Sew rows together. Press seams open.

Press backing for quilt. Sandwich with batting and quilt top, baste, and quilt as desired.

Using an acrylic ruler and two carpenter's T squares on corners, trim the quilt using a rotary cutter to ¼" beyond the corners of the blocks. Bind.

SEATTLE SUMMER—
STILL RAINING
50" X 50"
Margaret J. Miller, 1997
Woodinville, Washington

The colors in this quilt seem richer than in some quilts because the quilt consists of Block B and its reverse. This project also features sashing strips of graduated widths that separate the blocks on point. The border triangles are, in effect, a field on which this sashing strip trellis is floating. Note how varying the width of the sashing strips can help bring the focus of the quilt to a certain area; in this quilt, to the center.

SEATTLE SUMMER—STILL RAINING

Additional tools required: 12" and 15" acrylic squares

Cut Block Size: 6½"   Finished Block Size: 6"

Number of Blocks Required: 40 blocks (4 B Blocks, 8 Mirror Image B Blocks, 16 Reverse B Blocks, 12 Mirror Image Reverse B Blocks)

Yardage

For the blocks, choose twelve fabrics from two color families with a value movement such as light to dark, or light to dark to light again. Let one color family predominate and intersperse three or four fabrics from the other color family into the dominant family.

Once you have selected your twelve fabrics, divide them into six stacks (see photo on page 11); Stack 1 would be your lightest fabrics, Stack 6 your darkest.

Stack 1 (Fabrics 1 and 2) and Stack 6 (Fabrics 11 and 12): ½ yard each

Stacks 2, 3, 4, 5 (Fabrics 3-10): ⅜ yard each

Sashing Strips: ¾ yard

Setting Squares: ¼ yard

Border/Corner Triangles: 1 yard

Backing: 3 yards (or less if you piece leftovers as part of the backing)

Binding: Your choice, depending on whether you use straight or double bias binding

Cutting Triangles and Wedges

Triangles: Values 1 and 6

See page 11, To Cut Triangles.

Stack two fabrics from Stack 1 (or from Stack 6) together, folds and selvages parallel. Slit folds up about 6". Crosscut 5½". Subcut five 4" segments from this 5½" wide strip. Cut resulting rectangles corner to corner.

Wedges: Values 1 and 6

You will be cutting wide wedges only for these two fabrics. Stack two fabrics from Stack 1 (or from Stack 6) together, folds and selvages parallel. Slit folds up a little more than 9". Crosscut a little beyond 9" of fabric. Trim to 9".

Subcut six 3½" x 9" rectangles. Cut wedge angle as per general directions on page 13.

Wedges: Values 2, 3, 4, and 5

Taking each stack in turn, place two fabrics on top of each other, folds and selvages aligned. Slit folds up a little more than 9". Crosscut a little beyond 9" of fabric. Trim to 9". Subcut three 3" x 9" rectangles, and three 3½" x 9" rectangles. Cut wedge angles as per general directions on page 13.

Sewing Blocks

Lay out triangles and wedges in order on a nearby table or spare ironing board. Make the blocks listed above under "number of blocks required," following the general procedures presented on pages 21-22.

Make one type of block at a time. First make four B blocks, press and trim them, and put them on the wall in their proper place, following the diagram. Next, make eight mirror image B Blocks, etc. Don't forget to alternate a wide wedge with a narrow one as you are assembling them for the block. Also, keep the straight-grain edge on top as the pair of wedges goes through the sewing machine. Most importantly, every so often take a pair of wedges off the top of the stack you are sewing, and put them to the back of their like-width stack, to mix up the fabric combinations you are sewing together.

Block Rotation

Sashing Strips

The sashing strips are graduated widths, and can be rotary cut. Cut the following sashing strips, and put them in place on the design wall following the diagram.

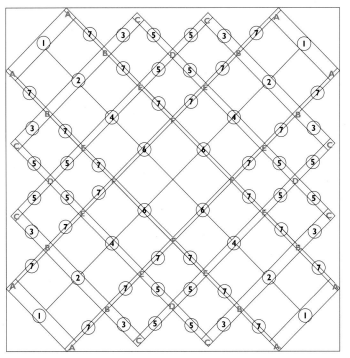

Sashing and setting square placement.

Fold fabric selvage to selvage. Slit the folds. Keep the fabric layers together.

Crosscut one 13½"-wide strip . From this 13½" strip, subcut through both layers:

Two 2½" x 13½" strips (#1 above)

Two 2" x 13½" strips (#2 above)

Two 1½" x 13½" strips (#4 above)

Two 1" x 13½" strips (#6 above)

Crosscut two 6½"-wide strips. From these 6½" strips, subcut through both layers:

Four 2" x 6½" strips (#3 above)

Eight 1½" x 6½" strips (#5 above)

Twelve 1" x 6½" strips (#7 above)

Setting Squares

The setting squares (or, in some places, rectangles) for this quilt can also be rotary cut. Fold fabric selvage to selvage; slit the fold.

Crosscut one 1"-wide strip. From this double fabric strip, subcut through both layers:

Four 2½" x 1" strips (A above)

Four 1½" x 1" strips (E above)

Two 1" x 1" strips (F above)

Crosscut one 1½"-wide strip. From this double fabric strip, subcut through both layers:

Four 2" x 1½" strips (C above)

Two 1½" x 1½" strips (D above)

From the rest of the fabric, rotary cut a 2" x 4" rectangle. From the 2" side, subcut four 1" x 2" strips (B above).

Border and Corner Triangles

Since I used a striped fabric on which the stripe was printed on the bias, I had to cut the triangles individually so the stripe would be placed where I wanted it.

If you use a more conventional fabric, cut two 15" squares out of your *folded* fabric (for four layers). Cut these squares corner to corner; the result is 16 triangles (you need only 12).

To make the corner triangles, you could:

1. Sew two of the triangles cut in the previous step together for each corner (you would obviously need to cut three 15" squares to begin with).
2. Cut two 10" squares in half corner to corner, or
3. Piece the corners as I did using the following procedure:

Cut a 4" strip of the inner corner fabric, a 2" strip of the border stripe; sew together. Put right sides together, align seams.

Using the 45-degree line on your rotary ruler, cut a 45-degree angle. Pin. Sew, then press seams open.

Measure up and to the right 10" from the right angle corner; mark. Cut between marks across the triangle. Center over the corner sashing strip of the quilt; sew.

Before committing to the arrangement of blocks on the wall, consider how different your quilt might look by rotating some of the blocks in place. The diagrams below were made without sashing strips, but they are the same blocks that you have on your design wall. In the first set of diagrams, the center four blocks were rotated.

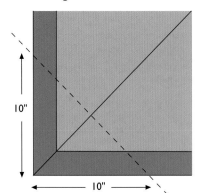

Piece the strips for the corner triangles.

Measure up and to the right 10" from the right angle corner.

Block placement with center four blocks rotated.

When the eight blocks just beyond the center four are also rotated, the quilt is hardly recognizable as the same as the quilts pictured above.

Block placement with the eight blocks just beyond the center four rotated.

This quilt can also be made without sashing strips, in case you would prefer to make it that way.

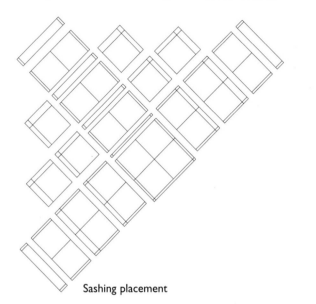

Block placement without sashing

Block Rotation

B Blocks

Reversed B Blocks

Sashing placement

Sew one sashing strip to each block. Sew a setting square to the sashing strip on the adjacent side of block. Do this to each block so the (now larger) blocks on the design wall look like this:

Quilt Construction

Join the blocks into rows; to sew border triangles, align inner corner of triangle with corner of block. The triangles have purposely been cut much larger than they need to be, so the whole quilt can be squared up after quilting. Sew the remaining two corner triangles to the quilt.

Backing

You should have a few wedges left over; you could assemble these into blocks and use them as the jumping off place for an interesting backing for your quilt.

Sandwich backing, batting, and quilt top, and baste and quilt as desired.

Using a long acrylic ruler and two carpenter's T squares, trim quilt using a rotary cutter to ¼" beyond first setting squares strips near corners. (Note that the sashing strips don't all end at the same distance from the border, because of the difference in the width of the sashing strips.) Bind.

guidelines for choosing
multiple color families

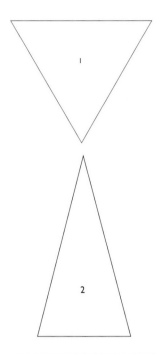

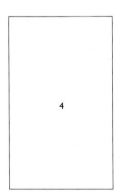

Shapes for use with Itten's system.

my color wheel is one of the more valuable tools I keep close at hand in the studio. Playing with the color wheel and tuning in to new combinations of colors that "fall together" on the studio floor accidentally certainly have supplemented the few formal color courses I have taken over the years. There are many good and inexpensive color wheels available on the market at any art supply, office supply, or university book store.

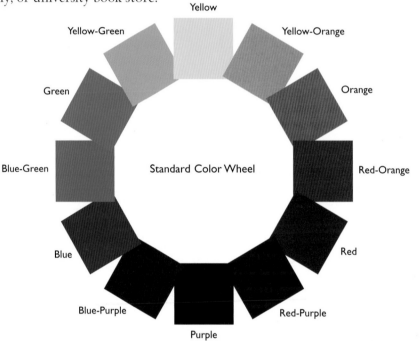

Johannes Itten is well known in the art world for the color theory he developed. His system for choosing harmonious color families is one I use often. With this system I can not only add to the colors I choose naturally, but I can also explore color groupings I've never worked with before. The information that appears below is certainly only the bare bones of this system. I encourage you to read and study color theory along with the techniques of quiltmaking that you learn from workshops and books.

If you wish to start simply, use complementary colors in your first few quilts. These are colors that are opposite each other on the color wheel, like green and red or orange and blue. If you select only two color families, try to expand the range of value you use in each color. Make yourself go all the way up to the lights, and all the way down to the darks.

To begin with Itten's system, trace (or photocopy) and cut out the four shapes, and superimpose them on the color wheel so the points of the shape fall into named color squares. Those colors indicated by the points of the shape are harmonious.

Shape number one, the equilateral triangle, can be rotated to find four different triadic color groupings. Shape number two, an isosceles triangle, can be rotated to select twelve different harmonious color triads.

The four-sided shapes will help you select pairs of complementary colors, which are called tetrads (four colors). Note that the square can be rotated to find three such groups, while the rectangle will help you select six of them.

Again, be conscious of the range of value (lightness or darkness) of the fabrics you choose. For many quiltmakers, even buying light fabrics at a quilt shop is a challenge! The most important thing is to enjoy playing with color. The more you play with it, the better you get at it. Remember that you are making quilts to please yourself and according to your own sense of color, which may or may not coincide with what your quilt guild approves of!

APPENDIX B pattern worksheets

In this section are worksheets that you can photocopy and use to do some of the design exercises in the book as well as to develop your own Easy Pieces quilt designs. It is sometimes more practical to cut up a paper pattern than to continually rotate blocks on the wall, such as when you are playing with offsetting rows from each other, or turning rows upside down.

Doodling quilting patterns is also easier and more effective on tracing paper placed over line designs, rather than staring at quilt blocks on the wall trying to imagine quilting patterns. If one quilting design doesn't seem to be going anywhere, you merely take the tracing paper off, replace it with a fresh sheet, and start again!

Remember to keep your reducing glass handy, as it will give you a better perspective on each photocopied paper design than looking at it with the naked eye. Sometimes you may see a pattern through the reducing glass that could be highlighted with color or value in the quilt.

The Blocks

Block A   Mirror Image   Block B   Mirror Image   Block B Reverse   Mirror Image

Groups of Four Blocks together

NOTE: You will be able to superimpose these designs on other patterns in this section. If you make full-size photocopies of this page, you can play with rotations of groups of four—all the same design, or two of one and two of another.

Groups of four blocks together.

 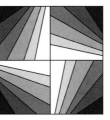 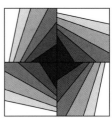 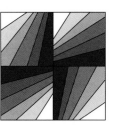

A Blocks   B Blocks   B Blocks   Reverse B Blocks

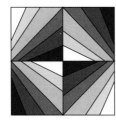 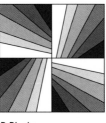 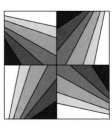 

A Blocks   B Blocks   B Blocks   Reverse B Blocks

 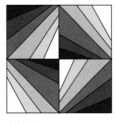 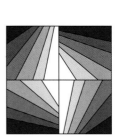 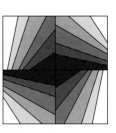

A and B Blocks   A Blocks and Mirror Image A Blocks   B Blocks and Reverse B Blocks   B Blocks and Reverse B Blocks

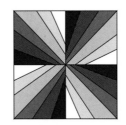 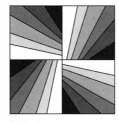 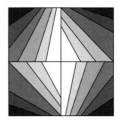 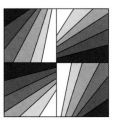

A Blocks   B Blocks   A and B Blocks   B Blocks and Reverse B Blocks

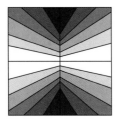 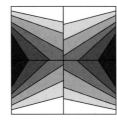 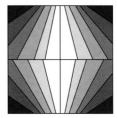 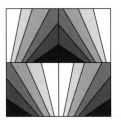

B Blocks and Mirror Image B Blocks   B Blocks and Mirror Image B Blocks   B Blocks and Mirror Image B Blocks   B Blocks and Mirror Image B Blocks

Pattern One *(See page 27.)*

A Blocks

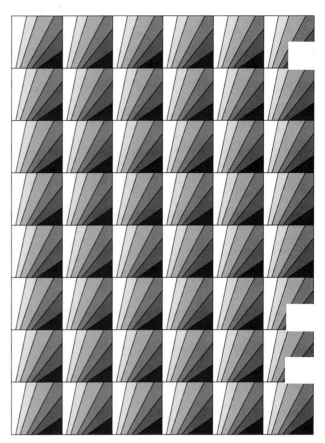

B Blocks

Pattern Two *(See page 27.)*

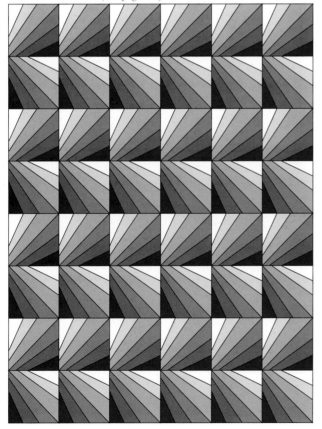

A Blocks

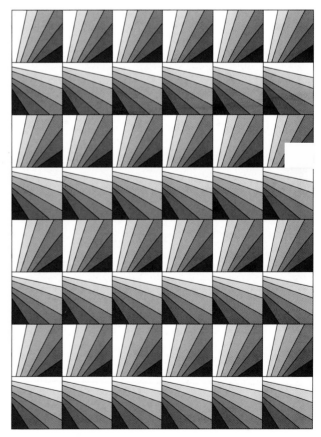

B Blocks

Pattern Three *(See page 28.)*

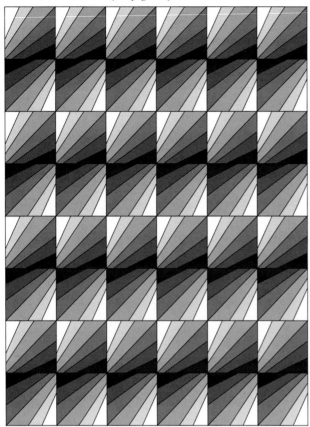

A Blocks

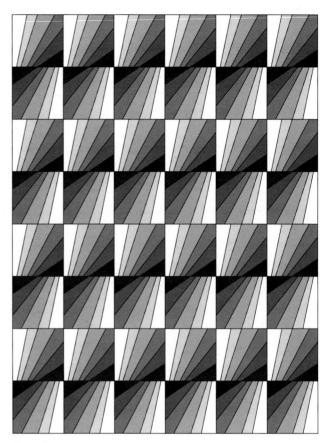

B Blocks

Pattern Four *(See page 28.)*

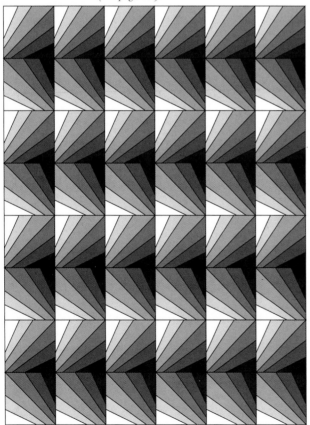

A Blocks

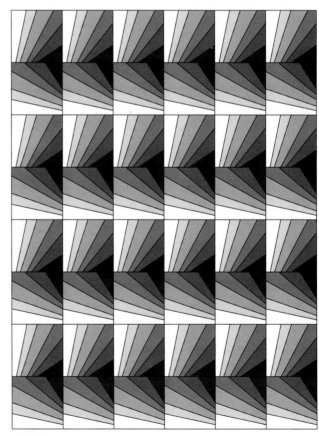

B Blocks

Pattern Five *(See page 30.)*

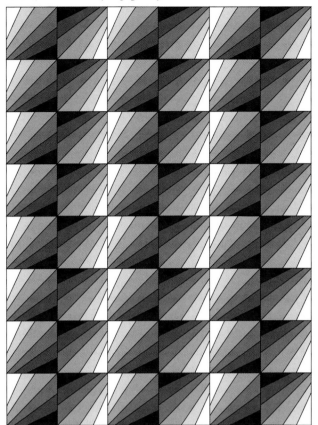

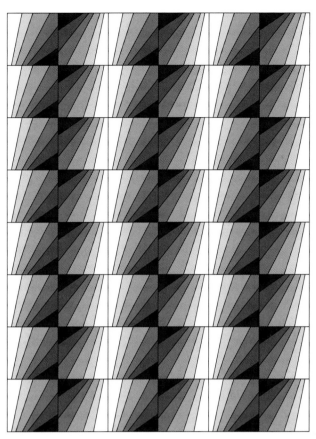

A Blocks

B Blocks

Pattern Six *(See page 31.)*

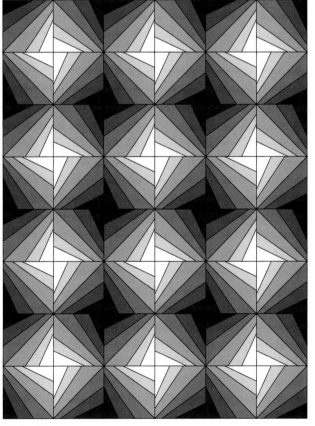

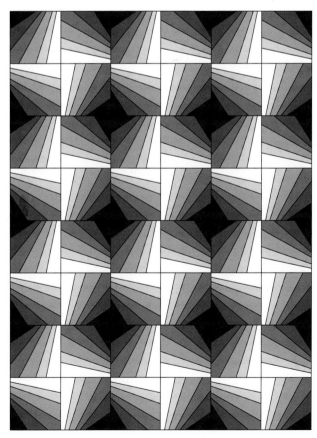

A Blocks

B Blocks

Pattern Seven *(See page 31.)*

A Blocks

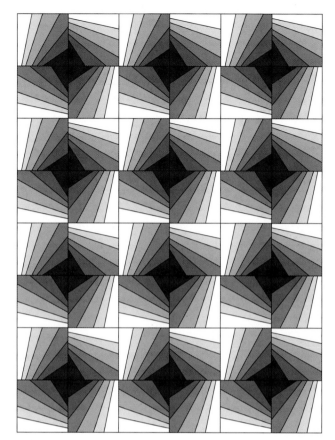

B Blocks

Pattern Eight *(See page 35.)*

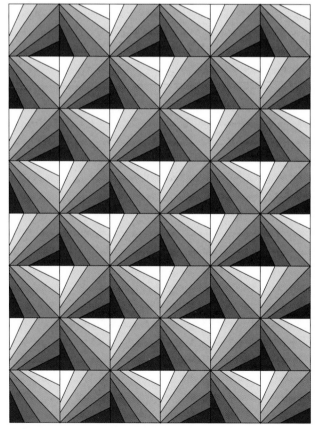

A Blocks

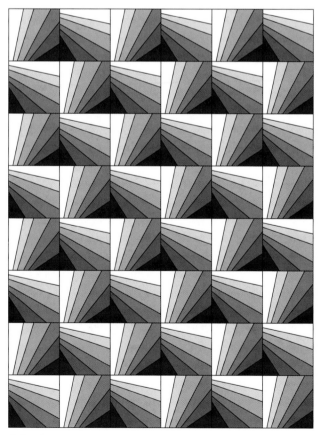

B Blocks

Pattern Nine *(See page 37.)*

A Blocks

B Blocks

Pattern Ten *(See page 39.)*

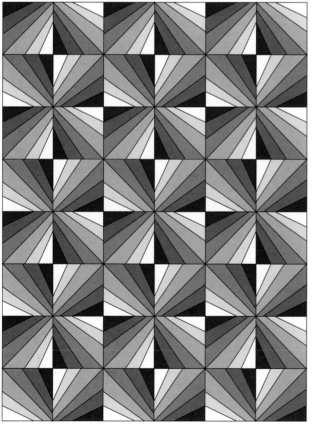

A Blocks

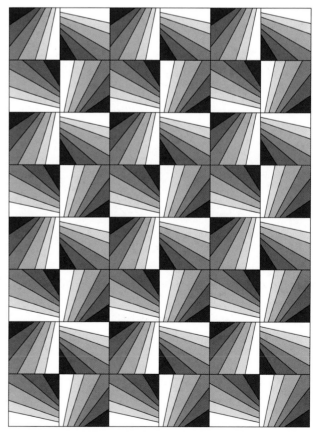

B Blocks

Pattern Eleven *(See page 41.)*

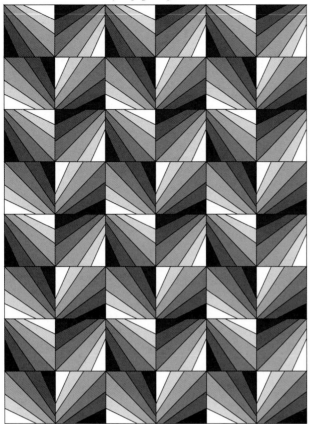

A Blocks

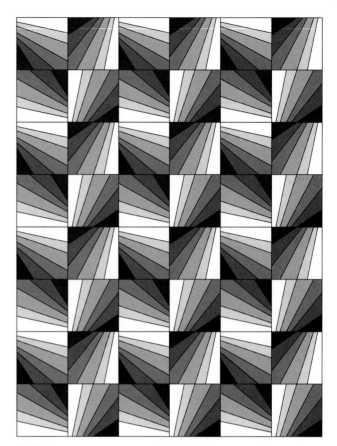

B Blocks

Pattern Twelve *(See page 42.)*

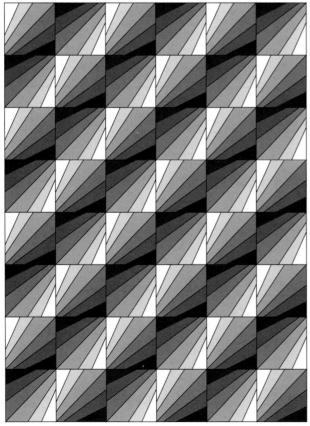

A Blocks

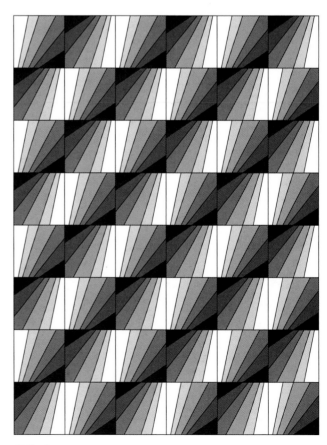

B Blocks

Blank Worksheets

The following worksheets are for you to use to sketch the wonderful designs you come up with using the arrow format. This kind of drawing of your quilt is helpful to use along with the photographs you may take of design experiments along the way. Both drawings and snapshots should be glued into your idea book to accompany notes you take on the making of specific quilts.

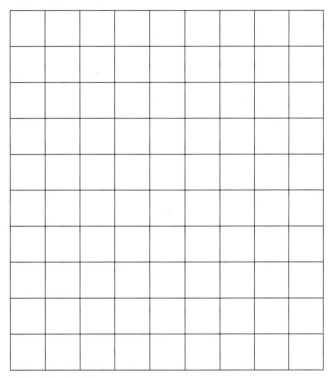

Blocks Used as Squares

Blocks On Point

Blocks Offset by a Half Block

afterword

The hardest part of writing any book for me has always been getting the sentences down on paper for the first time. But for this book, the hardest part has been finishing it! I literally had to hide my three-inch-high stack of photocopied designs to keep from adding just one more, to keep from playing with them while I was waiting for the tea water to boil, etc.! (This book was put together in its final form on my kitchen counter and adjacent dining room. There was not enough space on the table in the studio.)

The joy of writing a book like this is wondering where you, the reader, will take these ideas. Keep a camera and your idea book always within easy reach, and please send me snapshots of the quilts you come up with. I would love to see what new directions you take this most versatile of approaches to quiltmaking!

I am a big fan of those little calendars that have a new inspirational saying for each day, and one saying I've never forgotten is, "Originality isn't doing something no one else has done before, but doing it with new life and fervor." May your fervor, applied to Easy Pieces, bring you great JOY!

As I write these final words, I can hardly wait to get back into the studio and keep sewing. There are lots of leftover wedges and triangles both from the quilts and the "process photo" samples, and so many quilt possibilities swirling around in my head I'm not sure where to begin . . .

about the author

Margaret J. Miller is a studio quiltmaker who travels widely, giving lectures and workshops on color and design that encourage students to reach for the unexpected in contemporary quiltmaking. Her full teaching schedule has taken her throughout the United States, as well as to Great Britain, Australia, New Zealand, South Africa, and Denmark. Her presentations are known for their enthusiasm, humor, and sincere encouragement of quiltmakers at all levels of skill and experience.

Having done various forms of needlework throughout her life, Margaret learned to quilt and appliqué in 1978. At that time, she was on the faculty of the Home Economics Department at California Polytechnic State University, San Luis Obispo, teaching a creative textiles class. She later moved to San Diego, where she started Tanglethread Junction, a pattern business featuring appliqué and stained glass appliqué designs. In 1982 she sold her business as part of her commitment to becoming a full-time quiltmaker.

index

resource list

THE COTTON PATCH MAIL ORDER
3405 Hall Lane, Dept. CTB
Lafayette, CA 94549
e-mail: cottonpa@aol.com
(800) 835-4418
(925) 283-7883
A Complete Quilting Supply Store

ELECTRIC QUILT COMPANY
1039 Melrose Street
Bowling Green, OH 43402-3634
(800) 356-4219
All the designs in this book were first generated on the Electric Quilt 3 program . . . what fun . . .and what a time saver!

OMNIGRID™
P. O. Box 663
Burlington, WA 98233
(800) 755-3530
All cutting products from this company are of the highest quality and accuracy. They are available at most good quilt shops and fabric stores, and through quilter's supply catalogs.

MARILYN AND HARTLEY BADGER
Oregon Coast Quilting
P. O. Box 1085
Brookings, OR 97415
(541) 412-1002
Marilyn does commission machine quilting, and also teaches classes on using the professional quilting machines (in her shop, she has two different sizes for students to practice). Hartley invented an attachment called The Hartley Fence (patent pending) that enables professional machine quilters to quilt parallel diagonal lines and perfect circles!

PATSI HANSETH
Creative Machine Quilting
125 W. Spruce St.
Mt. Vernon, WA 98273
(360) 336-3014
Machine quilting on commission

MARK FREY, Photographer
P. O. Box 1596
Yelm, WA 98597
(360) 894-3591
Quilt photographer

SHARON RISEDORPH, Photographer
761 Clementina
San Francisco, CA 94103
(415) 431-5851
Quilt photographer

For more information on lectures and workshops by Margaret J. Miller, write to her at:
P. O. Box 798
Woodinville, WA 98072

other fine books by c&t publishing:

An Amish Adventure, 2nd Edition, Roberta Horton
Anatomy of a Doll, The Fabric Sculptor's Handbook, Susanna Oroyan
Appliqué 12 Easy Ways! Elly Sienkiewicz
Art & Inspirations, Ruth B. McDowell, Ruth B. McDowell
The Art of Silk Ribbon Embroidery, Judith Baker Montano
The Artful Ribbon, Candace Kling
Baltimore Album Legacy, Catalog of C&T Publishing's 1998 Baltimore Album Quilt Show and Contest, Elly Sienkiewicz
Crazy Quilt Handbook, Judith Montano
Crazy with Cotton, Diana Leone
Curves in Motion, Quilt Designs & Techniques, Judy B. Dales
Deidre Scherer, Work in Fabric and Thread, Deidre Scherer
Elegant Stitches, An Illustrated Stitch Guide & Source Book of Inspiration, Judith Baker Montano
Everything Flowers, Quilts from the Garden, Jean and Valori Wells
The Fabric Makes the Quilt, Roberta Horton
Fantastic Figures, Ideas & Techniques Using the New Clays, Susanna Oroyan
Focus on Features, Life-like Portrayals in Appliqué, Charlotte Warr Andersen

Forever Yours, Wedding Quilts, Clothing & Keepsakes, Amy Barickman
Free Stuff for Quilters on the Internet, Judy Heim and Gloria Hansen
Hand Quilting with Alex Anderson, Six Projects for Hand Quilters, Alex Anderson
Heirloom Machine Quilting, Third Edition, Harriet Hargrave
Impressionist Palette, Gai Perry
Impressionist Quilts, Gai Perry
Jacobean Rhapsodies, Composing with 28 Appliqué Designs, Pat Campbell and Mimi Ayers
Judith B. Montano, Art & Inspirations, Judith B. Montano
Mastering Machine Appliqué, Harriet Hargrave
Michael James, Art & Inspirations, Michael James
On the Surface, Thread Embellishment & Fabric Manipulation, Wendy Hill
Patchwork Persuasion, Fascinating Quilts from Traditional Designs, Joen Wolfrom
Piecing, Expanding the Basics, Ruth B. McDowell
Plaids & Stripes, The Use of Directional Fabrics in Quilts, Roberta Horton
Quilts for Fabric Lovers, Alex Anderson
Quilts from the Civil War, Nine Projects, Historical Notes, Diary Entries, Barbara Brackman
Quilts, Quilts, and More Quilts! Diana McClun and Laura Nownes

RIVA, If Ya Wanna Look Good, Honey, Your Feet Gotta Hurt..., Ruth Reynolds
Scrap Quilts, The Art of Making Do, Roberta Horton
Six Color World, Color, Cloth, Quilts & Wearables, Yvonne Porcella
Start Quilting with Alex Anderson, Six Projects for First-Time Quilters, Alex Anderson
Stripes in Quilts, Mary Mashuta
Trapunto by Machine, Hari Walner
The Visual Dance, Creating Spectacular Quilts, Joen Wolfrom
Wildflowers, Designs for Appliqué and Quilting, Carol Armstrong
Willowood, Further Adventures in Buttonhole Stitch Appliqué, Jean Wells
Yvonne Porcella, Art & Inspirations

For more information write for a free catalog from:
C&T Publishing, Inc.
P.O. Box 1456
Lafayette, CA 94549
(800) 284-1114
http://www.ctpub.com
email: ctinfo@ctpub.com